Generational Legacy

Dan LeLaCheur

Family Survival, Inc.
Eugene, Oregon 97402

All scripture quotations, unless otherwise indicated, are taken from the HOLY BIBLE, NEW INTERNATIONAL VERSION®. NIV®. Copyright ©1973, 1978, 1984 by International Bible Society. Used by permission of Zondervan Publishing House. All rights reserved.

The accounts of individuals and families are true, but most of the names and places have been changed.

Generational Legacy

1st. Printing

Copyright © 1994 by C. Daniel LeLaCheur
Published by Family Survival, Inc.
Eugene, Oregon

ISBN 0-964-22860-2

All rights reserved. Permission must be secured from the publisher to use or reproduce any part of this book, except for brief quotations in critical reviews or articles.

Printed in the United States of America

To Mardell, my beloved wife and friend of 40 years,
who always has the courage to tell me
when I'm wrong,
and the patience to put up with me
when I'm right.

To Clarence and Kate, Dad and Mom,
bestower of roots—and faith.

To Danell, Lynne, and Mark—our children,
the delight of our lives,
we grew and learned together.

And Jeffrey and Jonathan, our sons-in-law,
who join in this legacy.

To Ryan, Brandon, Jordan, and Nathan— our grandsons,
may our mount up with wings as eagles;
run and not be weary;
walk and not faint.

We have been blessed by each of you—
And we pray that you will have
"an endowment of the power of God's
goodness and favor."

Contents

Commanded To Bless
Introduction: Discovery

Part I
The Covenant and Curses

Part IV
Father—The Man He Was Meant To Be

Commanded To Bless

by Henry I. Drewfs, Jr.
Ret. Brigadier General, U.S. Army

Hank served his country for thirty years in the U.S. Army. He rose to Brigadier General before his retirement in 1990.

Hank had various commands and staff positions in the U.S., Europe, and Viet Nam. His last position as Brigadier General was Chief of Intelligence for General H. Norman Schwarzkopf just prior to Desert Shield/ Desert Storm in the Persian Gulf.

Hank and his wife Sharon became Christians in 1979, and he became an active member of the Officers Christian Fellowship, an evangelistic association for the officers within the U.S. military. He grew up in Portland, Oregon, and has always wanted to come back to his home state. The Drewfs now reside in Bend, Oregon.

Two years ago neither Sharon nor I knew anything about "generational things" such as curses or blessings. Now we have had the opportunity of not only learning about these things, but of passing on the blessing to each of our children, grandchildren, and our parents as well.

We were able to bless each one of them in a way we had never done before.

In retrospect, it is evident that the Lord used these two years to prepare us to pass on the blessing and that, in His perfect timing, He arranged a long-distance car trip to accomplish what He had laid out for us. Our family has been changed like nothing we have ever experienced before.

We first realized that there was something missing in our family when we heard evangelist Bob Laflin speak on the subject. Then Dan LeLaCheur came to our church, and in one of his sessions he encouraged parents to relate the stories of their lives to their children—especially their encounters with God.

Then it seemed as though the subject of blessing and curses was everywhere. We heard it in sermons, read it in Christian books, even came across it in discussions with relatives we hadn't seen in years. The Lord clearly had our attention. We began looking into the past in order to discover as much as we could about our families' spiritual backgrounds. On the positive side we found one of the original Puritan families in America, a circuit-riding preacher from New England, and a devout pioneer woman. On the other side was an occult practitioner and abandoned and abused families. We now knew it was our duty to somehow capture this information for the benefit of our three children, but we had no plan as to how we would pass it on to them.

God soon provided the opportunity. We began planning a trip to Georgia for the birth of a new grandchild. A plane trip from Oregon would have been the most economical and convenient way to go, yet somehow we felt the Lord wanted us to make the long drive instead. By doing so we could visit Sharon's parents in California and our son and his family in Texas, and with God's help we could perhaps mend some broken spiritual fences along the way. We were delighted to learn that our other daughter would be taking a break from work in Colorado and would be visiting Georgia while we were there.

Having presented the opportunity to see them all, God then graciously gave us further instructions as well. We heard that Dan LeLaCheur was coming back to Christian Life Center of Bend to speak. The spirit urged us to delay our trip to attend his sessions. We delayed our trip for two days, knowing that God had sent Dan back at just the right time. You can well imagine that Sharon and I took extensive notes as he explained the scriptural basis of passing on the blessing. His subject was, "How to bless your children."

We felt that God gave us a mandate after that service with Dan. We were convinced that He had literally commanded us to go and bless our family.

The trip itself was an unforgettable spiritual journey. Our church in Bend, Oregon, was fully aware of what the Lord was doing, so they sent us off as if we were missionaries.

Traveling across the country mile after mile, Sharon and I prayed, meditated, and even sang praise songs as we moved from one family location to the next. It was an intensely spiritual time as God revealed more and more truths to us. Some were truths from our immediate past and some from generations past.

God gave us wonderful discernment how to pray so that the hearts of each individual would be prepared for the breaking of curses and the starting of blessings. We both felt the anointing power of the Holy Spirit to fulfill the command to bless and, with the new insights we were receiving, the power to break generational curses as well.

Throughout the trip our prayers were quickly and abundantly answered. It became increasingly apparent that God had indeed planned the trip and that we were operating on His perfect timetable.

Sharon felt that she had never received the blessing as a child, so she knew to get it started she must bless her parents. When she prayed for her mother, her mother immediately began to respond by relating story after story from generations back. The capstone came the next morning when Sharon was able to lead her mother to the Lord.

I have never felt more perfectly in the will of God than I did in Texas and Georgia during the moments it took to pass on the blessing to our three children and five grandchildren, including our newest grandchild who was born after we arrived.

The Holy Spirit gave me words to use and prayers to offer that I am sure will have eternal meaning. Giving each blessing early in the visit lent a supernatural, peaceful, and meaningful quality to the time spent with our far-flung family. The results of that 7,400-mile trip has produced far more than we ever hoped.

I thank God for the gracious way He has chosen to deal with our family and my wife and me.

Introduction
Discovery

So Jellybean was never heard from again. His brothers, Marcus and Jeffrey, set out to seek their own adventures, but they always wondered where their naughty brother, Jellybean the possum, could have gone."

"Tell me that one more time, Papa. Please?" my grandson Jordan raised expectant eyes to me. "Tell me about Jellybean again! Oh! Look Papa! There he is!"

I slowed the car down as we crested the hill. Jordan strained against his seat belt to catch a glimpse of the infamous possum that decorated the center of the street. At the beginning of the summer, the poor animal had been run over by a car and left in the middle of the roadway.

Our first reaction was of sadness that the little creature did not make it across the street. Then that turned into repugnance as we drove by daily.

We watched the progress of his decay all summer long. Day by day we expected the street cleaner to remove his hapless body, but instead, the possum dubbed "Jellybean" became a target for unsuspecting traffic. His carcass became flatter and flatter until "Pancake" would have been a more fitting name to this victim of night blindness. Surely he would soon be scraped from the road and taken to wherever it is that these animals are taken. Yes, it looked like Jellybean had sadly been overlooked by the city office in charge of deceased rodents and various wildlife.

Anyway, it made for interesting conversation between myself and my ever curious seven-year-old grandson. Many a question and many a laugh was spent over stories about the disobedient Jellybean.

Then, one late summer evening, my wife rushed into the house and announced, with laughter rimming her voice, "You will never believe what happened to Jellybean today! You know the city truck that paints lines in the streets? Jellybean now has two yellow stripes running right up his back!"

Well, of course, we all had to pile into the car and rush down to see Jellybean's newest episode. We had a good laugh and continued to watch this scene until the fall rains came and finally dislodged the possum and he disappeared. Consequently, his flattened shape remained stenciled in the yellow street paint as a reminder of his story. The next spring, when the lines in the center of the street were painted again, Jellybean became nothing more than a poignant memory.

The street cleaners never bothered with that poor little possum until he had just become an unsightly mistake in the middle of the road. Instead of correcting or cleaning up their mistake, they simply painted over him.

We all have our own dead possums. There are those thoughts or actions that we know we should remove from our lives, but we get so used to them that eventually they become a part of the landscape, and we just paint over them as if they never existed.

My Search For Answers

All my life I have been an observer of people. Why does one person laugh at my joke and another one think it inane? Why will one person eat broccoli with a faraway look in his eyes, while another person can hardly bear to even pronounce it? Why does one person respond to the love of God and accept Jesus Christ as Savior, but the next person turns away, looking for another kind of savior?

The big question that motivated my search for truth was, why do so many families and individuals appear to begin a dedicated relationship with Christ, but end up in disaster? Not only do they often experience spiritual failure, but frequently go on to lead lives of frustration, pain, and disorientation. Like other Christians, I would tend to place the blame on *their* sin. I would observe the individual's circumstances and would even try to excuse his lack of real victory and spiritual power because of his current situation.

Yet, I fully know that God's plan is to bring all of us into the highest relationship with himself. In doing this, He gives us sound minds and clear spiritual senses of well-being and direction. (2 Timothy 1:7). In spite of all that, some do not experience this blessing. Why?

Having been a pastor for more than thirty years, part of which was spent in third world countries as a missionary, I was confronted by people who were obviously demon possessed. I saw firsthand the length to which Satan could and would go to injure and destroy God's highest creation. Still I knew that many people who were struggling so desperately to maintain their balance, overcome deep frustrations and defeats in life, were believers and were not demon possessed.

Questioning this problem, I stopped asking the question, "Why do some Christians go through such turmoil of soul? Instead, I started asking, "Why are other Christians definitely blessed and living victoriously for Christ? Why has our own family seen fruit for the Kingdom in all the living descendants of my parents?"

When I rediscovered the Abrahamic Covenant, my eyes suddenly fell upon an age-old principle, and the pieces of the puzzle began to fall into place. I began to understand not just what would happen to Abraham's seed when they kept the Covenant, but what happens to faithful believers today. I also saw what happens to those who take themselves out of the Covenant blessing and reject God.

This book is for all of you who may have a "Jellybean" or a dead possum in your life. You may have become so accustomed to it, so accepting, even unconscious of it, that you have painted over it with a facade of religiosity, good works, or self denial. I believe that by understanding the Abrahamic Covenant and God's new covenant through Christ, you will be set free from those thoughts and actions that keep you from the promised blessing of God.

Is it possible that you have not been able to experience the "joy of your salvation" because of a generational curse? My prayer is that through this study, you will find real deliverance and that the Holy Spirit will triumph victoriously in your life.

Part One
The Covenant and Curses

Based on the Abrahamic Covenant, God has given Abraham's seed and all Gentiles a promise. Included in the promise is a blessing or a curse. The curse can be passed from generation to generation. It can be stopped and broken by taking several steps. This includes the dynamic power of Christ's deliverance.

Chapter One

The Status Quo Must Go
The Abrahamic Covenant

*H*e had lived a long life. As he climbed the stone trail to the altar, Abraham thought about all that had passed between him and his Friend over the years. The higher he climbed, the more his heart quickened with anticipation. He had lived long, gone far, and was weary. Now, he was going to speak directly with the Lord.

Years ago, Abraham would have leaped the rocks and boulders strewn in his path as if they were nothing. He still felt the zeal, but was astonished at how his aging body answered his commands with only plodding progress. His

Lord was waiting, and the climb was only partially accomplished.

Stopping suddenly, Abraham convulsed with a deeply felt chuckle.

"What a fool I am!" he gasped. "If I cannot make it to the altar, I know the Lord will meet me wherever I am."

Lowering himself to a hollowed rock, he rested his back in its mossy coolness. "My Lord and my God," he whispered, "I wait for You here."

Throughout his entire walk with God, Abraham had never had a reason to doubt His presence. The Lord and he were friends. They trusted and honored each other. He and the Lord had a covenant together, and Abraham intended to keep it. They walked and talked daily. Abraham learned what was right and just. And in learning those truths, he promised the Lord that he would direct his children and his household after him to keep the way of the Lord. Yes, he knew God would meet him where he was.

Picture Abraham as the father of a large family. See him as one to whom a promise of highest value is given—a promise for his generation, but also for a thousand generations! That promised blessing is inherent upon all generations if they will obey and follow God. If they do not, they step out of the blessing into the judgment of God. Then the results of blessing turn into the consequences of a curse. *"Do not be deceived: God cannot be mocked. A man reaps what he sows. The one who sows to please his sinful nature, from that nature will reap destruction; the one who sows to please the Spirit, from the Spirit will reap eternal life"(Galatians 6:7-8,* NIV*).*

The Covenant Blessing

"I will make you into a great nation

and I will bless you:
I will make your name great,
and you will be a blessing.
I will bless those who bless you,
and whoever curses you I will curse
and all peoples on earth
will be blessed through you."

Genesis 12:2-3

"As for me, this is my covenant with you:
you will be the father of many nations.
and the god of your descendants after you.
No longer will you be called Abram.
Your name will be Abraham,
for I have made you a father of many nations.
I will make you very fruitful:
I will make nations of you,
and kings will come from you.
I will establish my covenant as
an everlasting covenant
between me and you
and your descendants after you
for the generations to come,
to be your god and the god
of your descendants after you.
The whole land of canaan,
where you are now an alien,

> *I will give as an everlasting*
> *possession to you*
> *and your descendants after you:*
> *and I will be their god."*
>
> Genesis 17:4-8

While reading the Abrahamic Covenant found in Genesis, understand that God's call to Abraham is a cry from His heart to His people. The human condition, because of sin, prompts God with this critical redemptive initiative. Not long before this time, the people erected the Tower of Babel. The building of the Tower revealed the condition of man's heart. Their defiance of God's plan seemed at first to be progressive, but eventually deteriorated. The tower collapsed, their language was confused, and eventually their rebellion brought them under God's judgment. The call and covenant given to Abraham was God's response to a human need.

The Hebrew word for *covenant* is "berith," and the Greek word is "diatheke." For our consideration both words mean "a last will and testament." God's gracious proposal to Abram showed His father's heart and what He wanted to do for His children. All the promises in both the Old and New Testaments are declarations of His will for His people.

God's Promises To Abraham

All Hebrew history begins with Abraham.[1] The genealogy in Matthew 1 traces Christ back to Abraham. He holds the historic honor of being the father of the Jews. The Jews claimed, with pride, that they were Abraham's children (Matt. 3:9).

There are eleven significant promises in the Covenant

that God made with Abram:

1) Abram's name would be great. (It would change from Abram to Abraham.)

2) A great nation would come from his seed. (Sarah his wife would bear a son.)

3) His blessing would be so great that all families on earth would be blessed through him.

4) To him and his seed Palestine would be an everlasting inheritance.

5) The multitude of his seed would be as the dust of the earth.

6) Whoever blessed him would be blessed, and whoever cursed him would be cursed.

7) He would be the father of many nations.

8) God would be a God to him and his seed.

9) His seed would possess the gate of his enemies.

10) Kings would be born from him.

11) The Abrahamic Covenant would be an "everlasting Covenant."

Abraham's Move To Greatness

Two outstanding traits mark Abraham's life from the moment he encountered God: He *obeyed* God and he *believed* God. From then on he moved steadfastly like a magnificent spiritual giant. He left his home and his family to follow the call of God. It is true Abraham demonstrated his human weakness, when he was willing to sacrifice the honor of his wife, Sarah, for his own safety. Yet, as the progenitor of his people and the very archetype of God, he moved by faith in a world of unseen realities, and into eternal greatness with his Covenant God.

God had told him, "*As for me, behold, my covenant is*

with thee" (Genesis 17:4). This is what God does: Today, He offers His covenant to us, and as far as He is concerned, it is done *(Galatians 3:29).*

When people enter this Covenant and keep its requirements, the Covenant is then established. God will always keep His oath-bound responsibilities and make good His promises.

The Covenant—a Family Matter

God, through Abraham, would generate a seed of blessing in all the earth. God would, in return, receive a universal spiritual family with obedience and faith like Abraham's. What satisfaction Abraham must have received knowing that from his obedience and faith a river of blessing would flow to the ends of the earth! It is right here that foreign missions originated.

This promise to bless all peoples on earth continues through the Old Testament. David particularly understood it, *"All the ends of the earth will remember and turn to the Lord, and all the families of the nations will bow down before Him. Posterity will serve him; future generations will be told about the Lord" (Psalm 22:27, 30).*

John 3:16 is the ultimate fulfillment of God's promise to Abraham. *"...Whoever believes in Christ will not perish..."* John the Revelator then writes the last chapter for us with such clarity and purpose. *"After this I looked and there before me was a great multitude that no one could count, from every nation, tribe, people, and language, standing before the throne and in front of the Lamb. They were wearing white robes and were holding palm branches in their hands. And they cried out in a loud voice: 'Salvation belongs to our God, who sits on the throne, and to the Lamb!'" (Revelation 7:9-10).*

Consequently the promises made to Abraham, reiterated by the prophets, the psalmists, and by Christ himself, will come to fruition on the Great Day of the Lord as prophetically witnessed by John. All mission efforts, every sacrifice of life, labor, and money, will be culminated in this glorious moment. People from every tribe, tongue, and nation will be gathered around the throne singing the praises of God.

It was God's full intention that the covenant blessing be projected through Abraham, to Isaac, to Jacob, to every generation, to this very moment when they are gathered around God's throne. The families of the earth were to bless their descendants and increase the blessing as it passed through the generations. *"Posterity will serve him; future generations will be told about the Lord. They will proclaim his righteousness to a people yet unborn—for he has done it."* (Psalm 22:30-31).

Blessing—the Key Word

Not only is a blessing promised in Genesis to Abraham's family, and in the Psalms to David's family, but it is promised to the spiritual children of Abraham throughout the world. Consider Abraham, *"He believed God, and it was credited to him as righteousness"* (Galatians 3:6). Recognize then that those who believe are considered adopted children of Abraham. The Scripture said that God would justify the Gentiles by faith, and announced the Gospel in advance to Abraham: "All nations will be blessed through you." Genesis 18:18). Then God verified His promise to Abraham and all Gentiles through Christ Jesus. *"He redeemed us in order that the blessing given to Abraham might come to the Gentiles through Christ Jesus, so that by faith we might receive the promise of the Spirit"* (Galatians 3:14).

In covenant making, it is imperative that the covenantor have the power to fulfill his legal obligations. We know that God used His supernatural power to make good His promise to Abraham. This was a supernatural covenant. Often miracles were necessary before the fulfillment of the promises were realized. The sustaining hope for the Jews who lived through 400 years of Egyptian bondage and slavery was the covenant promise of God to Abraham and his implicit faith. One of the most convincing examples of the validity of this covenant is that the Jews have never accepted the Abrahamic Messiah, yet their preservation as a race throughout the centuries is an absolute to the covenant and a living miracle every day.

The Abrahamic Covenant is a three-party covenant. God said to Abraham, *"I will establish my covenant between me and thee and thy seed after thee...for an everlasting covenant" (Genesis 17:7).*

In a three-party covenant, one party may break the Covenant but the other two parties remain bound to it. All seed of Abraham may not be believers and may not keep their part of the covenant, but they do not break God's covenant with Abraham. It is an "everlasting covenant." It has been in operation since the day God made it with Abraham.

There have been countless attempts through the ages to destroy the Jews. Hitler alone saw to the slaughter of six million on them. He would have done away with the whole race, but Abraham's faith in God's covenant promise prevented it: *"What I mean is this: the law, introduced 430 years later, does not set aside the covenant previously established by God and thus do away with the promise" (Galatians 3:17).* So the blessing was in the loins of Abraham, to be passed down from generation to generation.

In her famed Magnificat, Mary affirms God's covenant promise. *"My soul doth praise the Lord and my spirit rejoices in God my Savior."* She ends with these words, *"He has helped his servant Israel, remembering to be merciful to Abraham and his descendants forever, even as he said to our fathers."*

Is The Blessing Inherited?

Let us examine this idea to understand why I could not find reason for the drifting away of my friends and acquaintances from the blessings of God.

Tertullian's apologetic is as true today as it was when he wrote, "Christians are made, not born." Nevertheless, *Deuteronomy 29:29* is still a parent's promise: *"... but the things revealed belong to us and to our children forever...."* No one is automatically born again without accepting Jesus Christ as savior. Abraham's seed received a covenant promise. Children of all believers can enjoy the same benefits of the covenant blessing through Christ.

In describing salvation we often compare spiritual birth with natural birth. There is a distinct similarity, yet in considering the covenent blessing the two mesh into something more than separate experiences. Each affect the person. The spiritual affects the physical and the physical affects the spiritual.

We believe that a man is "born again" if he receives Jesus Christ into his heart. What does it mean? Is it the heart that is born again—the mind—the body—the soul—the spirit—the genes—the DNA? We are indeed a complex creation.

"Therefore if any one is in Christ, he is a new creation, the old has gone, the new has come" (2 Corinthians 5:17). If we know God's promise to Abraham, to his son Isaac, and to Mary is well-founded, that same promise is made possible to us by Jesus. We can then be certain that a real change takes place not only in one's spirit, but in every chromosome, every gene, even the DNA, when Christ makes us new. *"He is a new creation!"*

Therefore, when two spirit-filled believers come together to create new life, something spiritual, that has been living, and transferred from generation to generation for

4,000 years, takes place. When the sperm and the egg unite, more than a blob of protoplasm or viable tissue result. There is a *potential* heir to the throne in the womb. The promised blessing of God is the legal right of that unborn baby, of the small child, the mature adult.

The Other Side Of The Covenant

With the blessing came responsibility. The individual became accountable, the family was accountable. and the nation was accountable to the Covenant.

When individuals and families rebelled against God, they actually removed themselves from the promised blessing. They would not only suffer personally, but would invariably bring their whole family into disfavor.

Unless repentance and change took place, this would eventually affect the whole nation. The Hebrews would soon find themselves in some kind of slavery. Breaking God's Covenant means not only losing the blessing, but bringing upon one's self and succeeding generations a curse of indeterminate consequences.

In Joshua 7 Israel is routed by the men of Ai. Their leader Joshua is deeply distraught. He cannot understand why God has forsaken them. Then it is revealed that their defeat came about because of sin in camp. Achan had taken some of the plunder and hidden it in his tent. This act brought judgment upon the whole nation. *"Israel has sinned; they have violated my covenants" (Joshua 7:11)*. The sin of one man brought judgment upon the whole nation.

God's blessing for families is available today. But often a person or a family must remove a generational curse before the blessing can be fully obtained.

Chapter Two

Sins Of The Fathers
The Generational Curse

*M*ax Jukes, a known atheist, lived a godless life. He married an ungodly girl, and from this union there were 310 who died as paupers—150 were criminals, 7 were murderers, 100 were drunkards, and more than half of the women were prostitutes. His 540 descendants cost the state one and a quarter million dollars.[1]

Many of the problems of the present generation are linked to the sins of their fathers.

Fred spoke to me after a men's retreat in California. With tears flowing from his eyes and his voice quavering, he said, "I learned that my father is my grandfather." He then said that his main desire in life was to have a good family and to raise his children to love God. However, he was having a difficult time accepting himself and being a good husband and father because of what he knew.

Martha related how she had an extreme feeling of rejection since childhood because of physical and sexual abuse and names her parents had called her. She was in her late 50's with grown children and grandchildren. All these years her life had been uncertain and dismal because of the curse of rejection and abuse that had been placed on her as a small child. Tears streamed down her cheeks as she asked for prayer, "How can I break this feeling that I have carried for so many years?"

Bill, an accountant, told me of his distressing battle with lust. He shared how he had gone to peep shows and eventually had sex with a prostitute. Naturally, his sexual relations with his wife were at an all-time low. Bill was one of the most guilt-laden persons I have ever met. He was on the verge of suicide. He also shared how as a boy he had found his father's girlie magazines hidden in the garage. He would wait for his father to go to work so he could sneak out and look at them. The excitement of a boyhood addiction had turned into a lifestyle that was destroying him.

Don called long distance after he heard me speak, and said, "I need your help! You prayed with me at a certain meeting, but I never told you the whole story." Then he proceeded to tell me that several years ago he had been arrested and convicted of sexual abuse of children. He was released, but two years later he was arrested again for a similar offense, convicted and placed in prison for five years. He had now been out of jail for about five years. What grieved his heart most was that while all this was happening, he had a small daughter he was raising in his home. He spoke of her promiscuity during high school, and how it had continued into college. Now she was married, but had one affair after another. Don said, "I know I had a lot to do with her feelings, and her lifestyle. How could she be anything else after living with me? Now she is coming to visit me. How can I help her?"

People from all walks of life have shared similar accounts with me: pastors, leading elders, women, and many young people. They speak of a bondage, a sin, an attitude, a spirit that has kept them from the joy of their salvation.

I, the Lord your God, am a jealous God, punishing the children for the sin of the fathers to the third and fourth generation of those who hate me, but showing love to thousands who love me and keep my commandments (Exodus 20:5).

There is sufficient testimony by many that succeeding generations are blessed or cursed by the sins of their ancestors. Don, with the promiscuous daughter, Bill who became hooked on pornography because of his father, Martha and Fred are all so typical of the thousands who live under a generational curse.

Now, let us look at several ways in which a generational curse is transmitted.

What's In Your Genes?

There are certain physical characteristics that are passed from one generation to the next. Color of eyes, hair, or skin. These are not necessarily curses—unless you do not like that color. Often the genetic makeup of a person passes on tendencies to certain weaknesses that can be a physical curse.

My father suffered intensely with kidney stones in his

thirties and forties. I remember him lying on the floor, moaning and groaning with unrelenting pain. I had no idea what that pain was like—until I began to suffer from kidney stones myself. My doctors always asked, "Did anyone else in your family ever have kidney stones?" My youngest daughter, Lynne, has had to answer that same question.

Doctors tell us the tendencies for other diseases are often passed on from parents to children, such as, hemophilia and sickle cell anemia.

The Theory Of Natural Law

When God gave Abram the promised blessing, He covenanted with him that it would be everlasting to all generations. It was given in response to a people gone mad. Mad with rebellion and mad with sin; the people were seeking after their own desires. God's judgment had been experienced once, when He had sent the flood. The Tower of Babel was still fresh in His mind, and the sin of Sodom just over the horizon.

The dynamic in all of God's Covenant promises is that He will bless unreservedly all those who follow Him. He will bless:

The fruit of your womb.

The crops of your land,

The calves of your herds,

The lambs of your flocks,

He will keep you from disease

You will drive out your enemies.

(Deuteronomy 28)

The implication is that anything outside the Covenant promise, which included faithfulness and worship of Yahweh, would bring destruction and the curse of sin. The covering was not limited to a roof of blessing, but a roof of protection from outside forces of destruction.

This is based on the *Theory Of Natural Law* (or God's Law). Scientific laws are "natural laws." Remember, they are made by God and kept in place by Him. Laws of gravity, inertia, photosynthesis, all the principles that keep life in the universe alive and on time. Heavenly bodies like the sun, the moon, and the rotating earth on its axis are part of God's Law.

Whenever man interferes or rebels against these laws he comes out from under the roof of God's protective blessings. In so doing, he becomes a target to the destructive forces of natural laws. God declared to Abraham that if his people allowed this to happen they would come under a curse. *"If you ever forget the Lord your God and follow other gods and worship and bow down to them, I testify against you today that you will surely be destroyed. Like the nations the Lord destroyed before you, so you will be destroyed for not obeying the Lord your God"* (Deuteronomy 8:19-20).

The Nation That Forgot God

The nation of America is today experiencing the tragedy of forgetting *"the Lord your God."* The results are all around us. They are no different from what has happened to every nation from early Israel to the present. Some of the results are:

Sodomy tolerated by many as an alternate lifestyle.

The killing of a million and a half unborn babies annually through abortion.

Unbridled sex without responsibility for its consequences.

Mothers and fathers who have turned their back on their children.

A fifty percent divorce rate nationally.

Continued racism.

Dishonesty, lack of integrity, and selfishness in business and in politics.

A bitterness toward Christians, and an animosity toward the church and God that compares to the days when God destroyed those on earth.

Rage among many people—police beating the defenseless, gangs burning and looting, parents abusing their children, and children murdering their parents.

Rebellion is at an all-time high in America. *"Rebellion is as the sin of witchcraft" (1 Samuel 15:23).* Witchcraft is a stench in the nostrils of God. A rebellious people will soon self-destruct.

How Has Good Been Pushed Out?

My friend, John DeVries, the President of *Mission India 21*, has a theory of how God has been squeezed out of American society.[2]

Our country was founded on a God/man relationship that included God in every phase of American life. Most of the leading colleges in this country were started as religious schools. The laws of our land were based on the principles of the Ten Commandments. Even if people did not have a personal relationship with Christ, most everyone believed in God, and had a reverence for Him.

Then *rationalism* began to push out the abstract experience of faith, and as technology and industrialization developed, God became less "appropriate" in the community experience.

This eventually led to the *secularization* of our society.

Pluralism started to reach not only into the social fiber of communities, but into the religious thinking of the professors in the revered institutions of higher learning. It was not long before religion was separated from many areas of culture. If and when it was taught, the Bible was treated as a collection of fables or superstitions from an uncivilized past.

This naturally caused the rise of *agnosticism and atheism.* The growth of atheism grew from two percent of the population in 1900 to over 21 percent by 1985.

All gods must be worshiped, so Yahweh and Christ were sacrificed on the altar of *materialism.* We became a nation devoted to worshiping whatever gave us pleasure. The natural result of materialism in the 60's and 70's led the country into *secular humanism.* This says, "I am all the God that is necessary; therefore I do not need an invisible God. I will worship myself."

In a general way, God has been pushed out of our society. He also has been pushed out of some of our churches, and sad to say, many of our homes. We have become a nation living apart from the Covenant promises, and the results are in keeping with God's warning to Abraham, Joshua, Nehemiah, Isaiah, and the early church. We are a people searching for answers. Many who rebel and are angry, blame God for their condition.

The regressive steps of each generation away from God and into sin is the progression God warned the Hebrew fathers about. The sin of one generation is multiplied many times over by each succeeding generation.

Somehow, Satan has deceived this nation so badly that we have forgotten several thousand years of history, and the great moral, philosophical, and religious traditions. Our society is faltering so much that it seems completely unable to pass on the moral teachings to the next generation.

In the 1960's I sat with nearly 400 University of Washington students in a large hall on the Seattle campus. We watched as guru Dr. Timothy Leary appeared in his completely white outfit. He mesmerized impressionable students as he placed a candle on a table. He then crawled up behind it, crossed his legs and folded his hands and said repeatedly, *"Turn on, tune in, drop out."* For an hour and a half we listened to him extol the benefits of LSD.

His influence contributed to change the course of this country. Its effect is still felt in the succeeding generations of parents, high school teachers, and college professors who never knew what hit them in their search for the god of the great "high." Timothy Leary believed that control of the American consciousness was the issue.[3]

Secret Sins Shouted From The Housetops

The Secret Sins of One Generation Will be Committed Openly by the Next

The hippies of the 1960's introduced an utopian, acid-induced lifestyle. Flower power and astrological predictions were in vogue. The 1970's brought us the therapies of the *human potential movement*, which shook America loose from its traditional values of the past 200 years. This has led to widespread experimentation with mystical powers and an occult wave that is methodically destroying millions of souls each year.

A recent Gallup Poll revealed that 23 percent of adults and 28 percent of teens in America believe in reincarnation. Sixty-six percent of American adults profess to have had some psychic experience. Remember the scripture *"Rebellion is as the sin of witchcraft"* (1 Samuel 15:23).

Jeremiah 31:29 says, *"The fathers have eaten sour grapes and the children's teeth are set on edge."* Living outside the blessing always opens one up to the foremost device of Satan—a satanic influence following through from one generation to the next.

The sad commentary of this scenario is not just unregenerate parents producing unregenerate children. It is parents who have taken the blessing of God and the salvation of Christ for granted. A whole nation of Christians have played fast and loose with the people of Canaan. They have accepted the gods of this world, sacrificed their children on the altars of materialism, success, and acceptance. In so doing, they have stepped out from under the promised blessing into the promised curse. Remember, *the secret sins of the fathers will be done openly by their children.*

"Only one life - twill soon be past. Only what's done for Christ will last." You know the poem. It sounds so good. In fact, there may be those who think it is a quote from the Bible. But it is not scripture, nor is it entirely true! Sin also lasts; until it is confessed it goes on and on, sometimes for generations. *"...punishing the children for the sins of the fathers to the third and fourth generation..." (Genesis 20:5).*

Chapter Three

Ghosts In Your Attic
Family Spirits Follow A Generational Line

*L*aVonne attended our church. She was a striking beauty who had a sad story to tell of her early life. She had been raised in London, and some of her earliest recollections were of the war. She related to us how the Germans would bomb the city during the night and she and her sister would go out each morning and look for bodies. What an impression placed upon a young mind! She also revealed that both her mother and grandmother were deep into the occult. She remembered them as having strange and sometimes frightening powers of fortune-telling and witch-craft.

She then shared with us that her mother and grandmother had both sensed that LaVonne had these occult powers lying dormant in her life. They told her that someday she would have even greater power in the spirit world than either of them. Now that I have a better understanding of the generational progression, I believe they had transferred their satanic powers to LaVonne. The day came when she literally opened herself to the spirit of Satan.

Not long ago my wife was visiting in the city where we pastored and saw LaVonne on television, predicting the fortunes for a call-in audience. She had become one of the leading witches in this city. I have often wished that I had been equipped to deal with that situation before she completely yielded to the spiritual powers of her ancestors (called "familial spirits").

The typical progression is that these spirits of the occult will transfer to the children of the same sex, in this case the daughter or granddaughter. At times the spirits will move over to the opposite sex line of the family. The spirits claim the right to remain in the family based on unresolved sins. This is the reason God, in *Deuteronomy 23:3*, commanded the Israelites to *"not receive"* an Ammonite or Moabite into their Holy place until up to the tenth generation. This was to make sure they had been completely cleansed of the spirit that had possessed them. In their religious ceremonies they sacrificed their own children, and practiced divination and fortune-telling.

Now, let us assume that LaVonne's children are believers and are serving God. They must break that spiritual connection! If it is not broken there will be a significant amount of oppression and resistance to the joy of their salvation in their lives.

Demons—
on The Inside Or The Outside

Who Can Be Demonized?

Christians who are under the blood of Christ are safe from being eternally lost. It is obvious from Scripture that a believer is subject to the pressures and influences of Satan that affect him in many outward manifestations.[1] They cause oppression and negative feelings about one's faith. A person in this state of mind and spirit often becomes critical and uncertain of God's leading. This is the reason Paul urges the believer in *Ephesians 6:11* to *"put on the whole armor of God so you can stand against the devil's schemes."*

These influences and attacks are what I call being demonized, from the Greek, meaning, "have a spirit," but not "possession." Possession means complete ownership and control which would conflict with the surrendering of one's spirit to Christ.[2]

To be demonized[3] then, is to come under the influence rather than the indwelling of Satan. The Christian is veritably beaten up, pummelled, and attacked physically, mentally, and spiritually. It can be compared to a virus that attaches itself to a human body. It weakens. Physically, it can be very painful. Mentally, it causes depression. The word "influenza" comes from a Latin word meaning, "a blast from the stars." I think the word demonized means, "a blast from Hades."

My experience, and that of many whom I have interviewed, is that Christians are not demon possessed. I do not believe that God and Satan can inhabit the same person. I do know that Satan vies for the body as well as the soul of all of God's creation, especially His children. Satan demonizes those in a generational line where there has been spirit activity. So he comes like a virus, trying to contaminate, weaken, and pollute our minds with negative thoughts and motives. He is like an hired assassin. He continually beats on his victims until they lose the joy of their salvation. This joy is not a surface happiness. This is what the scripture means when it says *"the joy of the Lord is your strength"* Nehemiah 8:10.

These generational spirits will remain to torment unless they have been dealt with directly. Our position in Christ is certain and without question:

"When you were dead in your sins and in the uncircumcision of your sinful nature, God made you alive with Christ. He forgave us all our sins, having canceled the written code, with its regulations, that was against us and that stood opposed to us; he took it away, nailing it to the cross. And having disarmed the powers and authorities, he made a public spectacle of them, triumphing over them by the cross" (Colossians 2:13-15).

Those of us who have been in the trenches of life know that we have that confidence in Christ and his atoning grace of which the Scripture speaks. We also know that Satan never lets up on the converted. Ephesians 6:16 urges us to *"take the shield of faith, with which you can extinguish all the flaming arrows of the evil one."*

There is a marked difference between forgiveness of sin, and the consequences of sin.

A person can be forgiven of their sinful past, but still face a life of compulsive behavior, emotional abuse or damage, and the memories of sinful hurts.

Occult practices can be forgiven as easily as the smallest sin. But, demonic familial spirits will not give up without a supernatural confrontation. Therefore, they will often harass or keep a believer off-balance, which in essence, keeps that one from the joy of his salvation. These spirits must be dealt with directly. It is easy to put theology in neat little packages, but life must be dealt with as it really is, not as one would like it to be.

1 Thessalonians 5:23 says, *"May God himself, sanctify you through and through. May your whole spirit, soul, and body be kept blameless at the coming of our Lord Jesus Christ."* There is a difference between these three entities. The spirit may be blameless, but the soul or body is actually under tremendous attack by Satan.

Spiritual Protection

Any family with an occultic progression can break that line and have complete victory. However, if it is prevalent in any relative, or if there has been dabbling in spiritism of any kind, the children need to be physically and spiritually protected.

Spiritual protection calls for binding of those familial spirits, and building a hedge of protection around the life. A continual communion with Christ by prayer, Scripture reading, and receiving of the Lord's Supper is needed.

Physical protection means removal of the child from the individual who has the familial spirit. Never let such individuals babysit or be alone with the unprotected child. God is able to free any person from a familial spirit, but until He does, that spirit will continually try to affect every member of the family.

You may have questioned why God instructed the Israelites under Joshua to go into the Promised Land and completely annihilate the people who lived there. This was not a population problem, but a spiritual problem.

> *"When you enter the land the Lord your God is giving you do not learn to imitate the detestable ways of the nations there. Let no one be found among you who sacrifices his son or daughter in the fire, who practices divination or sorcery, interprets omens, engages in witchcraft, or casts spells, or who is medium or spiritist or who consults the dead. Anyone who does these things is detestable to the Lord, and because of these detestable practices the Lord your God will drive out those nations before you. You must be blameless before the Lord your God"* (Deuteronomy 18:9-13).

God knew what would happen naturally with the men of Israel and the women of the other tribes. They would intermarry. Soon they would be worshiping other gods, sacrificing their children, and practicing sorcery. He knew this would contaminate the nation and they would come under the curse of the covenant.

Does this sound like America today? The worshiping of other gods, sacrificing of children, and practicing sorcery? God's covenant was an *everlasting* covenant. The same promises that the Jews received through Abraham have been operating these thousands of years.

A blessing was inherit in the Covenant upon the sons of Abraham and all succeeding generations. I propose that there was also a curse passed from generation to generation upon those who did not keep the Covenant.

Jeremiah understood this, as did all of Israel who passed down this prophecy, *"You show love to thousands but bring the punishment for the fathers' sins into the laps of their children after them"* (Jeremiah 32:18).

There is no statute of limitations on unconfessed sin. It does not die, nor does the Instigator of that sin allow it to cease having an effect without a struggle.

There were absolutes concerning generational circumstances. *"No one born of a forbidden marriage [illegitimate birth] nor any of his descendants may enter the assembly of the Lord, even down to the tenth generation"* (Deuteronomy 23:2). The lawgiver believed that it took ten generations for the sin of the parents to be washed from that lineage. *"No Ammonite or Moabite [children of Lot and his incestuous relationship with his two daughters] or any of his descendants may enter the assembly of the Lord even to the tenth generation"* (Deuteronomy 23:3).

These tribes were constantly at enmity with Israel and they were the ones who hired Balaam the prophet to place a curse upon Israel. Because of their acceptance of Israel the Edomites and the Egyptians could enter the sanctuary in the third generation. The Bible records the warning often that if fathers worship idols, their children will suffer.

Are You Who You Think You Are?

Think about who you are in relation to your family. I am not only Dan LeLaCheur, but I am Clarence LeLaCheur's son. I look like him. I act like him. I think like him. When he taught me how to hunt and fish, throw a ball, and drive a car, he taught me about himself. When he taught me how to love my mother, he taught me how to love my wife. When he related to me in discipline as a father, he taught me how to relate to my children. When he threw his arms around me and told me he loved me, he taught me how to love my children. When he shared his God with me, and called Him Father, I understood God to be like my father.

There are times when I sense my dad's presence in my life although he has been gone fifteen years. In my mind I can feel his tremendous effect upon my life. Many people are similarly affected by a generational curse passed on to them by their father. Children can feel the rejection, the hate, the abuse, the coldness all their lives.

I shall always remember the son who threw himself onto his father's casket and screamed obscenities. When I was able to quiet him, he sobbed uncontrollably as he said, "He never told me he loved me. He never put his arms around me. And now he never will." I watched this young father for several weeks afterward and noticed that he never held his children. He never told them he loved them. It was as though he were held back by a rope binding him. He had become the very person he hated in his father.

How many times have you heard people condemn certain traits in their parents, and then seen them display exactly the same characteristics? There are many genetic similarities in parents and children. There are physical characteristics as well as environmental responses that accompany this close relationship. There is also a spirit that flows from one generation to the next. That spirit can be tender, pliable, easily grieved, and sometimes wounded almost beyond repair.

I am not only Dan LeLaCheur, the son of Clarence, but I am the father of Danell, Lynne, and Mark. They are largely today what my wife, Mardell, and I are as parents. There is a spirit that flows through our genes as well as genetic physical similarities.

In the early years of our children's lives we are responsible for their general health. We provide shelter, nutrition, the proper immunizations, and medical care. We want our children not only to be physically healthy, we want them to be intellectually sound. We send them to school and we read to them. We help them learn math, social studies, and history. We want them to have social skills so we expose them to other people. When they have problems with playmates, we teach them how to deal with them in a give-and-take manner. We teach them how to face all the consequences of life.

Knowing there is a spiritual factor present in each child, we should also be as concerned with their young and tender spirit. As parents we have a tremendous influence on the developing of this spiritual persona in our child. David the Psalmist understood this. *"I will be careful to lead a blameless life. I will have nothing to do with evil. No one who practices deceit will dwell in my house. No one who speaks falsely will stand in my presence"* (Psalm 101:2).

If we are truly concerned about our children's health, we must be equally concerned for their physical, mental, and social health. We shape the spirit in the child by how we relate to them and teach them to relate to others and to God.

Most of us know the devastation physical, sexual, and mental abuse can produce later in life. Abuse of the spirit is as devastating as anything done to a child. Occultic activities, blasphemy against God, and idolatry of any kind produce a spiritually ill adolescent and adult.

Parents are role models in every way. I have heard parents say about their children as young as four or five: "I am going to let my child decide if they want to go to church or not." In so doing, that parent is saying that church is not so important that I want my child to go. They are letting that child know their own real value of church. If your child has a vitamin deficiency and the doctor prescribes a vitamin supplement you don't say, "I want my child to decide on his own whether or not he takes it. If he doesn't like the taste of it, he doesn't have to take it." We are intelligent enough to know that by doing so we would be inflicting physical harm on our child.

On August 31, 1992, the television program *60 Minutes* showed the grown children of several of the Nazi High Command during Hitler's reign of terror.[4] Their fathers had been responsible for the death of millions of Jews. These children, now in their 50's and 60's, are still bound by the unthinkable sins of their fathers. One woman stated that for over 40 years she has had to take sedation to sleep at night.

Hitler's closest aide was Martin Bormann. His son said that when he converted to Catholicism he had to forgive his father before he could become a Catholic priest. Another had married a Jewish woman, seeking to atone for his father's sins. Obviously this could not alone bring peace of mind. He said, "It's like running away, but my father always gets me. I cannot forgive him!"

These were living testimonies of the effect of the sins of the fathers upon their children. Every one of them were crying out against the sins of their fathers. Some knowing that before they could have peace, they must forgive them. Some not able to do so. All hurting tremendously.

As the study of Max Jukes revealed, certain sins are transgenerational. They are transferred by spirits from one generation to the next. Illegitimate babies often produce illegitimate babies. Children from divorced parents often repeat the same mistakes in their own marriages.

We have not seen all the results of the sins of the past two generations. The children of two generations ago are now becoming parents. I am convinced that *The Sins Of Succeeding Generations Surpass Those Of Former Generations.* Is it simply cultural? Or is it the result of a broken covenant with God?

When we consider the seriousness of the moral decline in America, we must put it into biblical perspective. When the Bible speaks about *visiting the sins of the fathers to the third and fourth generation,* the Hebrews understood it in their cultural context. As the birthright or inheritance was passed on, it was assumed that it would increase with each generation. Each blessing growing with each succeeding generation.

Generational influences multiply. A blessing becomes larger as it passes on, and a curse becomes magnified as it is relived in each succeeding family. *Sin begets sin.* There is a law of increasing returns with each generation.

I believe that much of what America is experiencing today is a direct result of the experiences of the generations born in the late 40's and 50's. During World War II, American young men left their homes for the first time. They went to the Far East, mid-East, Europe, and the islands of the seas. There they became involved with cultures and religions unlike their own, that were passed down through the generations. Many of these men had sexual relations with women of these diverse religions. Often these were deep into spiritism, Satan worship, and idolatry. Some of the Americans dabbled in these religions as well.

It is likely they brought back many of these spirits to this country through their close association with many of these pagan religious practices and their followers. According to *1 Corinthians 6:16* a man *"joined to a harlot is one body."* If these American men became "one" in the sexual experience with those who worshiped evil spirits, is it not possible that they too came under the same spirit influence?

These spirits began to transfer and multiply as generations reproduced. There may have been no conscious effort to avert these spiritual influences until they came into full bloom in the 60s, 70s, and 80s. The churches were certainly unprepared for this onslaught of satanic influence. In fact, they were more concerned about social issues than spiritual, and played directly into the hand of Satan.

We are now seeing the grandchildren and great-grandchildren acting out the sins of their forefathers. We have come to realize that in the past twenty-five years the moral values have completed the paradigm shift. There is a complete change of consciousness among this present generation.

Perhaps you are suffering the results of a generational curse that has never been broken. Your experience may not be generational, but if you feel harassed or oppressed by sins that have affected other family members, and you do not have the "joy of your salvation," consider dealing with the situation in a scriptural manner. A time of fasting and prayer, along with the support of your pastor or other persons who have experience in spiritual warfare may be the solution.

Please understand, every negative experience in your life is not a *curse*. A *curse is evil that comes through supernatural power*. Such as "the sins of the fathers," as we have mentioned, and submitting to demonic powers wilfully.

There are *attacks*, *tests*, and *lessons* that we all face. God allows these situations to help us define our faith, build character, and be examples to others. Examples of these are Daniel in the lions den, Paul's, "thorn in the flesh," Jacobs limp, and countless present-day happenings that most believers experience.

Jesus said, "*I have told you these things, so that in me you may have peace. In this world you will have trouble. But take heart! I have overcome the world*" (*John 16:33*).

Chapter Four

Breaking The Record
Breaking The Curse

Justin is a fine pastor who has seen God bless his ministry many times with real church growth. Justin's grandfather was into a series of religious philosophies. Eventually, he settled on a cross-breed of several occultic experiences. Justin remembers collecting the six or seven books that his grandfather had written. Later he burned them so they would not fall into innocent hands because of their false dogma.

His grandfather chose twelve women disciples to be his leaders and with whom it was alleged that he had committed various sexual practices. He also dabbled with the occult and became quite involved in spiritism. His son, Justin's father, became embittered over the whole scenario. He rejected his father and all religion, and became very materialistic. Death seemed to stalk this family. His sister died at birth, and his brother was drowned in the ocean. At the age of 44, after battling with depression and other self-destructive demons, Justin's father put a gun to his head and killed himself.

Justin told me how his father had prided himself in the fact that he was a self-made man, and that he had built his financial empire all on his own. He was arrested for bootlegging liquor but beat the charges. Then, at the age of 44, he came under severe spiritual attack. Having no godly resources to fend off the satanic forces, he committed suicide.

This was a devastating blow to a ten-year-old boy. Justin remembered how he lost weight and went through tremendous physical and emotional turmoil. Through his father's death, his mother and sister came to Christ and dedicated their lives to Him. Thirty-four years later, after Bible college and a very successful ministry, Justin experienced a very low time of life. He said it was like someone trying to beat him up every day, physically and spiritually. It was like catching a virus and having it consume his strength.

He realized now that he was exactly the same age as his father was when he committed suicide. His mother, who had seen the spiritual battle of Justin's father, and had watched him lose that battle, recognized that the same spiritual forces were attacking her son and trying to take his life. She identified it as an attack of Satan. She resisted and bound the spirits, and Justin found the victory and peace of the Lord in his life.

Justin later related that up to this time he had kept the writings of his grandfather as a kind of family heirloom. He thought that someday members of the family or someone else would be interested in reading them. Now, realizing the significant influence of that generational spirit, he destroyed the writings. To this day he has not been troubled by those familial spirits.

> *"Consequently, just as the result of one trespass was condemnation for all men, so also the result of one act of righteousness was justification that brings life for all men. For just as through the disobedience of the one man the many were made sinners, so also through the obedience of the one man the many will be made righteous"* (Romans 5:18-19).

> *"Therefore, there is now no condemnation for those who are in Christ Jesus, because through Christ Jesus the law of the Spirit of life set me free from the law of sin and death"* (Romans 8:1-2).

> *"Christ redeemed us from the curse of the law by becoming a curse for us..."* (Galatians 3:13a).

How Will This Help Me?

In your heart you may ask, "Isn't every sin, every curse of the past, forgiven at the time of my acceptance of Christ for salvation?"

Yes! Absolutely! You have already been forgiven. The price was paid. Redemption's plan is in effect, but I have become aware in working with believers over the years that Satan often continues his diabolical onslaught of "demonizing" individuals. Memories of hurts, abuse, mistreatment need to be erased. People of poor influence in our past need to be forgiven. Altars need to be built of praise and declaration of faith. The full armor needs to be put into place, so *"that we can stand against the schemes of the devil"* (Ephesians 6:11).

If you feel that you have been living under a generational curse, or that your body and soul are being demonized constantly, then begin to take the following redemptive steps:

Identify possible sources of oppression and satanic points of entry in your life.

Make a list of the sins, the sources of the sins if you know them, and how they are affecting you or present members of your family. Here are several known sources of generational curses:

Occultic practices	*Alcoholism*
Demonism	*Drug addiction*
Spiritism	*Sex perversion*
Ancestor worship	*Abuse*
Contacts with the dead. (Deuteronomy 28)	*Incest*
Anything having to do with blood sacrifices	*Fornication*
Most New Age culture	*Homosexuality*
T.M. and Yoga	*Murder*
Nature or animal worship	*Suicide*
Rape	

Commonly accepted attitudes and characteristics include:

Rage	*Bitterness*
Covetousness	*Greed*
Gossip	*Lying*
Lack of integrity	

Poverty can be a generational curse as well as obesity and certain types of deafness. There are countless psychological diseases that are passed down from generation to generation. It is possible that these and other traits may have passed from generation to generation. It is also possible that you have become involved in one or more of these sins that could be passed on to your children.

Regardless of where and how these curses came into your life, they need to be dealt with directly, scripturally, and as soon as possible.

Identification of generational sins in your life is imperative. You must know what sins you are dealing with and how to break their power. You also will be better able to obtain complete victory if you have been specific about what they are. After you have identified these sins and attitudes and dealt with them, destroy the list.

Confess your sin

"If we confess our sins, He is faithful and just to forgive us our sins and to cleanse us from all unrighteousness" (I John 1:9)KJV.

Sample Prayer: Heavenly Father, I confess my sins and failures to you. I pray that the power of (_____ fill in) be broken in my life and that I be cleansed in the blood of Jesus Christ who gave himself that I might be set free. Forgive me, and wash me from this sin now and forevermore. In the name of Jesus, I pray. Amen.

Receive the forgiveness of Jesus Christ, and the victory that we have through His sacrifice. Satan may come to you and try to convince you that you are still the same old person and that nothing has happened. Remember, he is a liar and a deceiver. You, as a believer, have the authority to claim *Romans 8:1* and *Galatians 3:13*. Practice making that assertion with boldness, and in the name of Jesus. Satan's grasp will get weaker and weaker.

What Is Repentance? Is it saying you are sorry? Is it weeping, shedding tears, and feeling terrible? Many people do not fully understand the meaning or depth of repentance.

Repentance is not a feeling; it involves *action*. The desired result of repentance is change. To only feel sorry will not bring about change. Remorse is not repentance. When the cycle of negative feelings and actions is broken, change takes place. Change in relationships occur as the feelings that produced aggression, hatred, jealousy, fear, and selfish anger are crucified on the cross. Without identity with Christ's crucifixion, memories and battle scenes will continuously be replayed.

Often counselors try to bring about healing in relationships by encouraging the counselee to change the way he or she acts or to repeat certain positive phrases. We know surface changes never last long. Man's carnal nature will always surface and repeat sinful actions.

Real repentance breaks the power of sin. Repentance results in forgiveness. Forgiveness is the total blanking out of the offense. It is not only a canceled note, but it is the canceled note torn in pieces and burned.

Confess the sins of your ancestors.

The act of confessing the sins of your ancestors is virtually a lost practice. Traditional Hebrews thought one generation was not only responsible for the next, but the succeeding generations were affected by the preceding generations physically and spiritually.

"But if they will confess their sins and the sins of their father—their treachery against me and their hostility toward me, which made me hostile toward them so that I sent them into the land of their enemies— then when their uncircumcised hearts are humbled and they pay for their sin, I will remember my covenant with Jacob and my covenant with Isaac and my covenant with Abraham, and I will remember the land" (Leviticus 26:40-42).

"O Lord, God of heaven, the great and awesome God, who keeps his covenant of love with those who love him and obey his commands, let your ear be attentive and your eyes open to hear the prayer your servant is praying before you day and night for your servants, the people of Israel. I confess the sins we Israelites, including myself and my father's house, have committed against you. We have acted very wickedly toward you. We have not obeyed the commands, decrees and laws you gave your servant Moses" (Nehemiah 1:5-7).

This act of confession is very crucial in breaking the "familial" spirits' hold upon your life and the members of your family.

A girl I'll call Jennie was following the steps that I suggested to her, "Identify the sins and the ancestors involved. Those sins can no longer have a hold on your life or on your children's lives. Satan has no right to accuse you in any way. Jesus has paid for your victory."

As she mentioned each sin and the ancestors involved, her heart seemed to break and she began to weep. I could sense the agony and the pain of years being lifted. What an experience! What a cleansing! We could sense we were in the presence of Jesus and that Jennie was on a new road of peace and joy. After her prayer, she related, "I always felt the hurt. I knew something was there but I couldn't identify it and I did not know how to get rid of it."

As I had with others, I cautioned Jennie that Satan does not like what is happening here. He will come with his lies and deception and try to rob you of peace and victory. Be ready to stand on the authority of the Word, the Blood, and the name of Jesus. Resist Satan and he will flee from you.

Sample Prayer For Confessing The Sins Of Ancestors:

God, I confess the sin of a lying spirit that has been in my family for generations. The spirit that was in grandfather James, my father Bill, and has shown itself in me. I ask for forgiveness for James, for Bill, and all of my ancestors who have had this spirit. I receive your forgiveness and cleansing from this sin. I pray that it will stop now and forever with my bloodline. I bind the spirit that comes from Satan in the name of Jesus. Lord, help me to be a person of integrity and truth. I pray this in the strong name of Jesus Christ. Amen.

When we pray for the forgiveness of our ancestors' sins it breaks the hold of their sins upon us. If they are living, God will only forgive their sins when confessed personally.

Forgive Your Ancestors

The next step may be very difficult, but it is equally important. Forgiveness is important for both you and your living relative. You must consciously forgive them. The memory that you have struggled with the most is the one most needing forgiveness. It may be sexual abuse, physical abuse, alcoholism, the pain of a broken home because of adultery. It may be unkind words, acts you were accused of, or painful situations you lived through and still may be living through. These are difficult to forgive. But they must be forgiven by you as well as by God. The generational chains that have bound you emotionally for years must be broken.

Forgiveness does not come easily. Especially if we feel we have been victimized and want someone to blame. But that very seldom eases our pain. Forgiveness releases the past. It is letting go of what we feel others, the world, or God has done to us. Celestial amnesia is releasing all the memories of the past except the love we have given and received.

Forgiveness stops the endless cycle of pain and guilt that we carry. We can begin to look upon ourselves and others with love. Don't wait! Forgive now!

Consciously Forgive Your Relative. If they are dead, you must forgive them before God. Verbalize it and weep over it. Let the anger, resentment, and fear go. If they are still living, go to them. Explain the bondage you have experienced, and explain what you are doing and why you must forgive them. This could be the most difficult action you have ever taken, but it will set you free. It will also set them free.

After your parents, aunts, uncles, or grandparents have also lived under guilt and condemnation when they suddenly realize that they have an avenue of freedom, they may ask you to forgive them. Do not be afraid to receive their confession or apology. Receive it gracefully if it comes; but if it does not come, continue in your act of forgiveness, and leave the rest to the Holy Spirit. If the best happens and they receive your forgiveness, give them a hug or a kiss. Pray with them. Defeat Satan at his ugliest game—the bondage of families. *"For if you forgive men when they sin against you, your heavenly Father will also forgive you. But if you do not forgive men their sins, your Father will not forgive your sins"* *(Matthew 6:14-15).*

There has been a rash of media stars revealing their past. I have watched as several have "come forward" with a revelation of sexual abuse or physical abuse. I have seen on television as they have confronted their father or mother.

Some parents have not received it. They have denied the allegations, refusing to appear on camera. My heart has gone out to both sides as I realize that this bondage could be broken through Christ. I remember shouting at the television screen, "Wait! Wait!" I said, "There is an answer. It is forgiveness." Instead of accusing, they must forgive to find real healing and love.

One sin that has hindered many people's prayers from bearing fruit is unresolved forgiveness. To forgive can be a very painful experience. Many of the people we need to forgive are not the most gracious, loving people in the world.

We must ask God to help us, then make the move. It may be painful to start the process, but the end result is blessing without measure.

Forgiveness stops the endless cycle of pain and guilt that we carry. We begin to look upon ourselves and others with love. Do not wait; forgive now!

> *"Therefore, if you are offering your gift at the altar and there remember that your brother has something against you, leave your gift there in front of the altar. First go and be reconciled to your brother; then come and offer your gift"* (Matthew 5:23-24).

> *"Therefore I tell you, whatever you ask for in prayer, believe that you have received it, and it will be yours. And when you stand praying, if you hold anything against anyone, forgive him, so that your Father in heaven may forgive you your sins"* (Mark 11:24-25).

The Roots Must Be Pulled Up. Jesus said to his disciples: *"Things that cause people to sin are bound to come, but woe to that person through whom they come. It would be better for him to be thrown into the sea with a millstone tied around his neck than for him to cause one of these little ones to sin. So watch yourselves. If your brother sins, rebuke him, and if he repents, forgive him. If he sins against you seven times in a day, and seven times comes back to you and says, 'I repent,' forgive him. The apostles said to the Lord, 'Increase our faith!' He replied, 'If you have faith as small as a mustard seed, you can say to this mulberry tree, "Be uprooted and planted in the sea," and it will obey you' "* (Luke 17:1-6).

The mulberry tree mentioned in Luke could live up to 600 years. Can you imagine the root system? One writer said that it might take 600 years to untangle the roots of this tree—they were so intense and intertwined. What Jesus is saying here is that a minute amount of faith could uproot this age-old, generationally bound tree, and cast it into the salt sea where it could no longer grow. Such is the power of faith.

The acceptance of Christ's forgiveness for sins of the past, will destroy the ancestral roots that have been entwined, physically, genetically, psychologically, and spiritually in a bloodline. The kind of faith and action that Jesus is talking about will not just cut off the branches and the top of the tree. It will pull up the very growth system that contains the curses of the past and will cast it into the sea of God's love and cleansing through the blood of Jesus.

Build a Hedge of Prayer Around Your Loved Ones.

The next step is to take the authority of your position as a Christian and begin to build a hedge of prayer around your life and that of your family's. *"I tell you the truth, whatever you bind on earth will be bound in heaven, and whatever you loose on earth will be loosed in heaven"* (Matthew 18:18).

Hosea did this for his wife Gomar. *"Therefore, I will block her path with thornbushes; I will wall her in so that she cannot find her way. She will chase after her lovers but not catch them; she will look for them but not find them. Then she will say, 'I will go back to my husband as at first...'"* (Hosea 2:6-7). She could not break out of the hedge of prayer, nor could her lovers break in.

Righteous Job prayed regularly for a "hedge" around his seven sons and three daughters. This hedge of prayer was so strong that Satan complained about not being able to touch Job or his family. *"Does Job fear God for nothing? Have you not put a hedge around him and his household and everything he has?"* (Job 1:9).

There is evidence that Job's children began to practice certain sins, and to have rebellion in their hearts. This is when the hedge was taken down and Satan was given the opportunity to bring physical destruction to Job's household. *"God honors His children, but rebellion is as the sin of witchcraft"* (1 Samuel 15:23). And God will, quite frequently, allow punishment to come upon the rebellious offenders. *"The Lord disciplines those he loves, and he punishes everyone he accepts as a son"* (Hebrews 12:6).

This prayer to build a hedge is often overlooked or comes only after serious problems with family. We need to learn its value and effectiveness early in our family life. It is not just an Old Testament practice, but the early church fathers knew its value and often incorporated it into their regular family altar times. The prayer binds the power of Satan and keeps him from demonizing you and your home. Do not hesitate to pray it often and in faith. Satan was defeated at Calvary and can no longer condemn you or take away the joy of your salvation.

Sample Prayer: Strong and Omnipotent Father, with your authority and strength I resist the devil in my life. I ask you to bind Satan in the lives of my family. I pray that you will build a hedge of protection around their minds, wills, emotions, and bodies. I ask that each member of my family will not only receive this protection from Satan, but each will be drawn to a very personal and close walk with you. Thank you for your strong presence in our lives. In Jesus' name. Amen.

Final Steps to Victory

1. Build An Altar

"(This altar) is to serve as a sign among you. In the future, when your children ask you, 'What do these stones mean?' Tell them that the flow of the Jordan was cut off before the ark of the covenant of the Lord. When it crossed the Jordan, the waters of the Jordan were cut off. These stones are to be a memorial to the people of Israel forever" (Joshua 4:6).

Write in your Bible the steps you have taken and the date. Details are not necessary, only the basic steps. Go back to this from time to time as a memorial altar. Praise God for setting you free from the generational curse that held you in bondage.

Teach your children the importance of building altars. Remember dates and places and events of salvation, baptism, healings, and answered prayer. Do not let them forget these important building stones. If they are very young, they will need to be reminded by accounts of the events. Make them exciting and build them into your chilren's lives as you do the ABC's or multiplication tables. If they remember these victories they will be able to face the future tests of Satan with faith and confidence.

Unbelief always vindicates Satan and makes God a liar. Faith always justifies God and proves Satan a fraud.

2. Prepare And Take The Lord's Supper

This is an act of complete obedience to Christ. It signifies His broken body, and the blood that was spilled at Calvary. It will help you remember that He did the work, not you. It was on the cross Satan was defeated.

You may want to wait to do this in a worship service at your church. You may ask a pastor to serve you in a special time of communion. You may want to do this with your family and share this breaking of the past with them.

3. Share This Experience

It is a good practice to share what you have done with another believer. Be sure to share it with your wife or husband or children. Verbalizing it will give you more ac-countability. Caution: Do not share with small children more than they can handle.

4. Tear Up The List

Now take the list that you made, tear it up, burn it, or throw it away. You are forgiven and cleansed. Do not bring it up again, (only in thanksgiving). It is under the blood of Christ. Remember, the new covenant has been sealed by the blood of Christ, but these steps are valid in appropriating His grace, and building a memorial altar.

Prepare for Blessing

If you have done all that has been suggested to merely get rid of the pain, you will be disappointed. That is not enough! A doctor knows very well that a patient who only wants the pain removed does not get well.

For eight years I had an unbearable pain in my side. The more I moved, stood, or ran, the more intense the pain. I went to several doctors. One thought it was psychological. One thought it was a serious disease, perhaps cancer. They were all willing to give me pain pills, and sometimes a shot of morphine when it was so unbearable that I had to be hospitalized.

Finally a kidney stone showed up on an X-ray. The specialist at the University of Washington Clinic removed it and I was a new man. For the first time in years, I was pain-free, no more symptoms. Most significant, however, was that the cause of the pain was gone.

I have suggested many elements that may lead to "disease" in your life. I have given you several steps for removing, not only the symptoms, but the sickness. Now is the time to make a total commitment to Christ. The world today encourages us to be self-centered, selfish, and demand our rights. This does not bring lasting freedom and joy. *Luke 17:33 says, "Whoever tries to keep his life will lose it, and whoever loses his life will preserve it."*

Now you can move on to a blessing that can be yours in this age of insecurity and hopelessness. A promised blessing for all times. *Those who prevail preserve their legacy for another generation.*

Part Two
Blessings

Balanced by the New Testament teaching of Christ, this present generation can receive and pass on blessing to the next generation. This was made clear to Abraham. He was the example of God's grace and love to a people who had drifted far from their heavenly father. The blessing can be ours—if we understand and follow God's leading.

Chapter Five

Get Ready - Get Set - Go!
Starting the Blessing
Part 1

*T*here is record kept of a great American man of
God. He was Jonathan Edwards. He lived at the
same time as Max Jukes (mentioned in chapter 2). But unlike
Max Jukes, he married a godly woman. An investigation was
made of 1,394 known descendants of Jonathan Edwards.
Thirteen became college presidents, 65 college professors,
three United States senators, 30 judges, 100 lawyers, 60
physicians, 75 army and navy officers, 100 preachers and

missionaries, 60 authors of prominence, one vice-president of the United States. Eighty became officials in other capacities, and there were 295 college graduates among whom were governors of states and ministers to foreign countries. Jonathan Edwards' descendants did not cost the state a penny.[1] Who cannot say that the blessings of parents pass from generation to generation?

Significant evidence abounds to verify the passing of blessing to one's children and future descendants.

What are the natural results of family blessing? What blessing awaits those who keep the new covenant provided by Christ? How can you put this blessing into practice in your home and in your life? You will see how God's promise to Abraham, and verified by Christ, is in reality God's plan for every Christian family.

> *Galations 3:14 says," He redeemed us in order that the blessing given to Abraham might come to the Gentiles through Christ Jesus, so that by faith we might receive the promise of the spirit."*

God's promises to Abraham were too dynamic to forget or misunderstand. In Genesis 17 the promise was to Abraham's descendants. He was 99 years old and his wife, Sarah, was 89. They had no children. Yet God proclaimed promises to Abraham that affect every generation for all time:

1. *You will be a father of many nations (vs 4).*
2. *Kings will come from you (vs 6).*
3. *This will be an everlasting Covenant for all your descendants (vs 7).*
4. *The land of Caanan will be yours and your descendants (vs 8).*

In Bible times it was customary for a father to pass down a blessing to his oldest son. It was a ritual that was important to the carrying on of the family wealth and heritage. Remember when Jacob stole his older brother, Esau's, birthright by deception? Esau was devastated. He cried out, *"Do you have only one blessing, my father? Bless me also, O my father" (Genesis 27:38).*

Once A Blessing Was Spoken, It Was Irretrievable. Esau did receive a partial blessing from his father Isaac, but it was not the *double* portion that was customarily given to the oldest son.

The Blessing Defined

The blessing in those days meant far more than receiving a monetary inheritance and possessions. It also spoke of the father's love, acceptance, and praise of the son. In essence, it proclaimed to the young man, *"You are pleasing to me, you are worthy of my trust, my lineage, my love, the profit of my lifetime, I am proud of you. I release you to be all that God wants you to be."*[2]

Whether or not a Hebrew son received his father's blessing had a tremendous impact on his future; for if he never received it, he was considered unworthy. There is an ancient Jewish maxim that says, *"The blessing of the father builds the children's house."*[3]

All children were given a general blessing, which was communicated specifically to each one. In today's Jewish society, bestowing a blessing upon the family is still practiced universally.

The Need For Blessing

There is such an innate need for a family blessing that many children suffer all their lives because they never receive it. Today the term "blessing" is used to describe an important emotional and psychological dynamic that transpires between parents and their children. This dynamic determines whether or not children grow up feeling that their parents, both father and mother, "speak well of them" or "praise" them, and, in short, give them their blessing. Though this blessing is not given through a ritual as it was in ancient times, it is given verbally and nonverbally throughout childhood and adolescence. By the time sons and daughters leave home to face what lies ahead in their future, intuitively they know if they have received that blessing or not.

Today cults deceive thousands of young people all over the world with counterfeit blessings. They give them the much-needed and sought after love and acceptance. Persons who have grown up without these family blessings are so hungry to be fulfilled that they are vulnerable to the counterfeits. False security, drugs, sex, and occult practices are offered as substitutes for what children did not receive from their parents. Consequently, they are left more spiritually destitute than they were in the beginning.

It is possible that businesses fail, marriages fall apart, future plans never materialize, and personal satisfaction in many lives is unfulfilled because the parental blessing was never given and received.

Fathers and mothers, there is no greater ministry available to you than the act of blessing your children. Children are prepared to "build their house," if, over the years, they have received the cumulative blessing of their parents. I am convinced that without the parental blessing, a foreboding sense of self-doubt and self-worth can stymie the basic building of a life of happiness and fulfillment. The mental and emotional health of adult children is contingent upon the blessing of their parents.

Chapter Six

Communicating
The Blessing
Why Is Touch So Important?

Part 2

The Hebrews and early Christians used certain symbols, gestures, and words in communicating the blessing. I have found the following to be of great significance in the process of modern family blessing.

1. *Significant Touch*...laying on of hands, hugging, kissing, a pat on the back to show comfort or approval.

2. *The Spoken Word*...A word of encouragement, a scripture, a prophetic word.

3. *The Raised Hand*...the symbol of receiving a blessing, the symbol of giving a blessing.

4. *The Handshake*[1]

The Significant Touch

Flesh upon flesh, skin to skin is a dynamic personal and powerfully significant act among humans.

In the marriage relationship, kissing, holding, and intercourse transcends verbal communication. It harbors a spiritual contact that is built into the very fiber of humanity. It is one of God's highest forms of communication or blessing between marriage partners. This is why the Scripture is so clear on avoiding premarital sex or joining oneself to a harlot. The act of intercourse in itself within the marriage relationship is beautiful and one of God's highest forms of physical communication. Outside of the marriage relationship, it is destructive, both physically and spiritually.

Each time a blessing was bestowed in the Old Testament, kissing, hugging, or significant touching took place. In *Genesis 27:26* Isaac said, *"Come near now and kiss me, my son."* History, reason, and experience tell us that the key to communicating personal acceptance, affirmation, and warmth is a significant touch.

In 1992, a study was done on the sense of touch in mothers of babies three months and younger. Seventy percent of the blindfolded mothers could pick out their own baby by the texture and warmth of the skin.

Touch verifies the information of the other senses, confirming what we hear, see, or smell. Touch confirms what it is, and where it is. Touch collects the information about our world.

Babies are wonderful to touch. They can be nuzzled, carried, cuddled, embraced. Babies are unceasing touchers themselves; they are explorers and learners, using sensitive fingers, tongues, and lips to confirm what they do not understand. And after babies explore, they run to siblings, parents, care-givers for an afffectionate touch or squeeze. We grasp hands, we hold hands, we shake hands. We hug, we pat, we reach out to others, and we receive in kind. Touch is the unspoken language of the human soul.[2]

Touch - The Outer Brain

German philosopher Immanuel Kant called the hand the "human outer brain." Hands provide a critical amount of knowledge about our world through the sense of touch. They can determine hot from cold, hard objects from soft, cotton from silk, and dimes from pennies. The trapped mind of Helen Keller was brought to life through the stimulation of her skin.[3]

We all have a normal human compulsion to touch. Have you ever been to an art gallery, and seen the sign "Do not touch"? Yet, the beautiful sculpture has an appeal that is only satisfied by touch. I empathize with children who are constantly told not to touch. They learn and grow through touch as much as through their senses of hearing, smell, and sight.

Touch - Our Social Communication

Desmond Morris, research fellow at Wolfson College, Oxford, has proposed a 12-step sequence of touching in courtship. It is a flow chart of physical intimacy and body accessibility. Each stage depends upon the couple passing through the previous stages. As the pair moves toward greater physical intimacy, each assumes certain touches are acceptable and expected. If a touch is not reciprocated, that also sends a message. Often couples, after marriage, take for granted the importance of the touching process, and therefore fail to satisfy one another completely.

The reciprocity of touch is also vital in the parent/child relationship. Many studies reveal that humans need a certain amount of stimulation to be healthy. There is a resurgence of discussion about the value of breast-feeding babies. Much of this centers not on the difference in the milk, but the amount of holding and cuddling that goes on between mother and baby.

Without any touch, children can die. As late as the 1920s, the death rate in the U.S. foundling homes for infants under one year was nearly 100 percent. In the 1940s, Dr. Fritz Talbot came back from Germany with the idea of tender-loving care for these children. He had gone to Dusseldorf where he visited a children's clinic. There he saw a large woman named Anna carrying a puny baby on her hip. The clinic director told Dr. Talbot that they too were losing babies systematically. When they had tried everything else, they finally turned the infants over to old Anna, who was always successful in bringing them around through cuddling, stroking, and cooing. The introduction of "mothering" in institutions dramatically reduced the mortality rates of these children.[4]

Recent studies have shown that premature infants who were massaged for fifteen minutes, three times a day gained weight 45 percent faster than those who were alone left in their incubators. The interesting fact is that the massaged infants did not eat more than the others. Their weight gain was directly related to the effect of touch on their metabolism.

Physical contact is the ultimate signal to infants and to small children that they are safe. Psychologists say children have many ways of telling parents they want to be touched. They are likely to cling and cry for help with activities they have been doing perfectly well themselves. Around age one, children frequently develop an attachment for a soft cuddly blanket, pillow, or toy, dragging it around with them, stroking and caressing it. It is there, providing the security of touch when the parent isn't. At about eighteen months, toddlers may exhibit separation anxiety and insist on parents' company, especially at bedtime.

Touch distinguishes "me" from "not me." Touch is important in forming a good self-image. The growth of that self-image begins as a child interacts with objects in the environment and the people he lives and plays with.

It is a sad fact that as children grow older, parents generally touch them less than they did during infancy and childhood. By adolescence, touch by a child's parents may be nearly terminated. Yet adolescents are eager for bodily contact, seeking to touch and be touched. This often creates a dilemma because they are becoming sexually mature.

Each year in the U. S. more than 1,000,000 girls under the age of twenty become pregnant and approximately 560,000 bear live children. The biblical ideal is abstinence; but our society has come up with less than biblical or Christian strategies to cope with this problem. Abortions, at 1.6 million a year, is the best answer they have been able to find. It is interesting to observe that many studies have indicated that being held or cuddled reduces anxiety, promotes relaxation and a feeling of security. This may be the reason sexual intercourse is often entered into by adolescent girls as a way to be held and cuddled.[5]

Being embraced often by a parent can help overcome feelings of loneliness and can generate feelings of love, reassurance, protection, and comfort. In a study on the connection between the wish to be held and depression, it was discovered there is a difference between males and females in respect to this need. Females wanted to be held at levels of depression, whereas males had the greatest desire to be held when they were not depressed.

The Healing Touch

The New Testament church knows the value of laying on of hands. Along with the obvious spiritual value, there is a physical benefit.

Deloris Krieger introduced this concept into nursing in 1975. She noted that the sick person became more relaxed, comfortable, and actually energetic when touched by others. She wrote that "an exchange of vitality occurs when a healthy person purposefully touches an ill person with a strong intent to help or heal." She said that the reason for this is that the hemoglobin level in the blood rises in the one being touched. The hemoglobin carries oxygen to the various parts of the body and brings healing. It was observed that pain reduced as much as 70 to 90 percent when the patient was touched by a caring person.[6]

It was found that even when a patient is unconscious, a strong physiological effect takes place when that person is touched by another human being. One researcher found during pulse-taking a significant heart rate change. Another found changes in blood pressure and respiratory rates in very sick patients whose hands had been held by nurses for as little as three minutes.

Some events, after 40 years of being away from home, are so imprinted within my mind that I shall always remember them.

My mother's hands were wonderful. I used to sit in church and look at her hands. I would memorize every line, the beauty of her graceful fingers, and the softness of her touch.

I was four years old when I came down with scarlet fever. My folks took me to the hospital where I passed out because of the excessive fever. Even now, after all these years, I remember the feel of a hand on my forehead when I finally woke up. I could tell without even opening my eyes that it was my mother's hand. Not only were her hands beautiful to a small boy, but I knew at an early age there was special healing in my mother's hands.

Norm, my brother, was probably thriteen, and I about ten when he got the great idea that he could fly on his bicycle. Evel Knieval was not the first to try it. Norm proceeded to pile up a few bed springs, then he laid boards up and over them. He said, "Now, Dan, if we pedal fast enough and come full speed onto the boards, the springs will launch us into the air and we will be able to fly." He was right. Anyway, he flew a few feet and landed without incident.

Being the typical younger brother, I proceeded to follow. Everything went as planned until I hit the boards on the springs. One of the springs popped up and grabbed one of the pedals of my bike. The bike stopped and I went flying through the air. I landed on my outstretched hands and immediately felt a searing pain around my neck. Struggling to my feet, I stumbled across the street to our house and fell into my mother's arms.

I shall always remember that scene as if it was being played out 50 years later. We had no doctor, we had no money for an emergency room. Neither was even considered. My mother laid me on her bed, put those healing hands on my collarbone and prayed for my healing. She then went to the old-fashioned icebox and brought me a dish of plain red Jell-O. I remember the Jell-O because we always had Jell-O when we were sick. I remember the prayer because we always had prayer when we were sick. I remember my mother's hands, because they were instruments of love and healing and were always available to her two sons and three daughters.

For over 50 years now, I have often put my fingers on a little bump on my collarbone. There has never been a time that I did not feel the warm presence of Christ my healer, and my mother's healing touch.

Let's take a look at the model of Jesus. *A man with leprosy came to him and begged him on his knees, "If you are willing, you can make me clean." Filled with compassion, Jesus reached out His hand and touched the man. "I am willing," he said, "Be clean!" Immediately the leprosy left him and he was cured. Mark 1:40-42.*

Here we see the typical response of Jesus. In that day, lepers were not touched by anyone, in fact, they were avoided. They were condemned to live out their days in loneliness and deprivation. They walked the countryside proclaiming their plight, "Unclean! Unclean!" Jesus broke the social barrier and touched the man. His was a healing touch, and the man was never the same again.

"People were bringing little children to Jesus to have him touch them, but the disciples rebuked them. When Jesus saw this, he was indignant. He said to them, Let the little children come to me, and do not hinder them, for the kindgom of God belongs to such as these. I tell you the truth, anyone who will not receive the kingdom of God like a little child will never enter it" *(Mark 10:13-15).* Jesus set a great example and shared a spiritual truth when he picked up those little ones and blessed them.

The Thankful Touch

Researchers have found that diners who are touched on the hand or the shoulder by a waitress tip better than those who have not been touched.

In vocational sessions, clients rated counselors who touched them as being more expert than those who did not touch them.

Students who were "accidentally" touched by library personnel when their library cards were handed back to them, gave both the clerk and the library higher "marks" than did a central group of students who were not touched.

A study group of 171 college students revealed that those who were touched by their instructor during individual conferences gave these instructors higher ratings. Those who were touched also showed a score of .58 higher than the untouched students.[7]

In competitive sports, researchers have found that winners give and receive more touches than losers.[8] A pat on the back or shoulder, or a high-five is like a gallon of hi-test gas. I remember a particular coach in high school. In the huddle, at the bench, or in a tense moment he would give me a pat or a thump, and I would feel a rush of adrenaline and be ready to play my heart out.

I, along with a group of American and Canadian pastors, walked down a narrow street in a rural India village. Although it was little more than an alleyway, there were people in various modes of activity: women washing clothes by hand, men engaged in serious talk, children, dogs, chickens, goats, and of course many holy cows everywhere. We were fascinated, almost to the point of being mesmerized. They, too, were fascinated by our white skin, blond heads, and western clothing. We were awed by the small one-room homes where as many as a dozen people lived, and the young children played with primitive toys.

This was indeed a once-in-a-lifetime experience, for we were about to see, for the first time, one of our literacy classes in action. I had helped raise funds to teach illiterate adult nationals in this country to read. This ministry is most effective in India because the Bible is the textbook. As a result, thousands of people become literate, and in so doing, are introduced to Jesus Christ at the same time.

I shall always remember this scene as long as I live: The group had gathered outside of one of the little one-room homes, which was the designated place for the first class of 30 women. I was busy taking in the sights, sounds, and smells of all our surroundings. Suddenly, a small wisp of a lady, dressed in her everyday sari, was standing in front of me. She looked up into my eyes, and said something in Hindi. I, of course, could not understand her. Then, she suddenly knelt before me, grasped my ankles in her two hands and began to kiss my feet. Embarrassed, I wanted to step back, but I was right up against the wall of the house, so there was no place to go.

I had not understood her spoken words, but the message of her touch and her expressive kissing of my feet spoke volumes. She was blessing me for bringing to her village the power of the printed page and the message of our Redeemer. Perhaps for the first time I began to comprehend what the Bible and its message really meant. I left that little village humbled, feeling the blessing of a poor woman's touch. The words that she could not make me understand in any other way were enameled upon my heart by a passionate touch of gratitude and hope.

The Blessing Touch

I remember many qualities of my father. When I was a small boy, I was sure that he was probably the strongest man in the world. He was not only physically strong, but also morally and spiritually stalwart. I never knew my dad to lie to me or try to deceive me in any way. He was not only a man of faith, but he was filled with hope. His preeminent desire was that all five of his children would serve God, and that if God so called, they would all be in ministry. Actually, there was little chance that any of his two sons or three daughters would be able to do anything else.

I was always convinced that God did whatever my dad asked in prayer. I had a healthy fear and respect of Dad. I feared him far more than I did God. When I was growing up, my dad's arms were longer than God's. His voice was clearer, and his discipline more expedient. And his "omnipresence" was physical. Through Dad I came to understand these characteristics of God. I also knew his love and tenderness. I saw my dad weep before it was okay for real men to cry. I felt his strong arms draw me to his huge chest as he would kiss me on the cheek. My dad was, indeed, God personified to this son. In fact, as I have written these words about him, I have found it difficult to keep from capitalizing the word dad in every case.

If my mother's hands were healing hands, my father's were hands of blessing. Dad grew up in the sandhills of Nebraska. In the late 1800s his parents had homesteaded a piece of land covered with soap-weeds, snakes, and sand. Dad became a typical frontier cowboy. It was a hard life, but I loved hearing my father tell of breaking horses, riding in the Fourth of July rodeos, and winning footraces at community gatherings. Many of the grandchildren of my father's parents would spend nearly every summer out at that same ranch where Dad had grown up. I would often imagine walking, working, and looking at the same scenes my dad experienced when he was my age.

Like many of that generation, Dad incurred countless injuries from being kicked by horses, or catching a finger or an arm in a primitive farm implement. Both of his hands had nerve damage. Not only were there fingers missing, but his hands shook quite severely. Yet, to a son who studied them by the hour, they were strong hands.

One of the keen memories of my dad concerns those hands. Whenever I had a pain, a broken bone, a toothache, or looked like I was running on less than all eight cylinders, I could count on Dad saying, "Son, we need to pray about that." Suddenly those unique shaking hands would come down upon my head with all the glory of an Abraham blessing Isaac, or David turning over his kingdom to Solomon. Now the hands were steady, they were strong, and I could actually sense a spirit of blessing and the presence of God. Even today I revel in those experiences of my father's touch.

How I thank God for my dad. He was not afraid to discipline. He was not ashamed to say, "Dan, I love you." He was never hesitant to throw his arms around me or put those hands upon my head and intercede for God's touch upon my life.

A man we'll call Jake came to the men's retreat, at which I was a speaker, with his father. He was in his mid-30s and I would judge his father to be between 55 and 60. Jake was big! Boisterous, animated! Yet, beneath his rough 'truck driver' exterior I could sense the little boy that is still resident in most of us men.

I spoke on the subject of fathers blessing their sons. I shared the power of hugging and touching our children along with that blessing.

While I was speaking about my dad, I noticed that Jake kept rubbing his eyes with the back of his hands. I also noted that his father would look at him, and then turn away; look again, then turn away. Following the seminar, several fellows came forward to pray and seek counsel. Just as we were finished, Jake appeared in front of me and asked me to pray for him, that he would be a better father. I sensed in my spirit there was more than he was telling me. I asked, "Jake, are you saying that you have a problem with your children?"

He said, "No, I just feel like I haven't done all I should. Something is missing."

Then I asked, "Have you blessed your children, Jake?"

A tear started down his cheek as he said, "I don't know

how; I don't know what it means; I don't know how it feels."

Just then his father was standing beside him. I instinctively knew that the problem was between the two of them. Neither Jake nor his father knew what to do.

I said, "Dad, is it time for you to bless your son?"

Jake fell to his knees in front of his father and for the first time felt the hands of his dad placed upon his head.

For the next twenty minutes the most beautiful scene unfolded. These were two men who loved each other dearly, but had never gotten past the cultural macho bondage far enough to bless or be blessed. They prayed—they cried—they laughed—they hugged—they became real!

Later Jake told me he felt like he had a 100-pound weight lifted from his shoulders. He said, "Now I know how it feels to be blessed. Now I know what I must do for my children."

Touch confirms the other senses of hearing, seeing, and smelling. In the touch there is significant healing. In the touch gratitude and warmth are communicated. In the touch blessing is felt in the process of communication.

Chapter Seven

Mom And Dad— Speak To Me!
More On The Blessing - The Spoken Word

*E*dgar Bergstrom was a successful contractor. But he was hit hard by the Great Depression of the 30s. In fact, he watched as his farm was taken away, and then his bank closed. He and his young bride lost nearly everything they owned.

Being a strong resourceful couple, Alice got a job as a telephone operator and Edgar landed a job with the WPA (Federal - Work Projects Administration). They continued to work hard until children began to come. Edgar learned fast and was soon a foreman. Then as times got better he struck out on his own as a road builder. It was not long until he was doing so well that they were able to buy a home and send the children to college. Edgar never forgot the hard times of the Depression. He was always afraid the bank would fail again. So he put most of his money in metal boxes and buried them in the woods behind their house. This was to be his children's inheritance. But he didn't tell his wife or his children where the money was buried. He always planned on telling them, but the time was never right.

It was July 4th. The family had just left the house after one of Alice's wonderful dinners that she'd become famous for. Edgar excused himself and went to his bedroom to rest. He told Alice that he felt a little worn out, and his stomach was a mite upset. About 30 minutes later Alice went in to check on him. She could not awaken him. Edgar died that day of a massive coronary. He was a fine man. His family and friends could not find a negative thing to say about him.

The last I heard, they were still looking for the money. They knew he had hidden it somewhere. They knew he planned to divide it up among his four children, but he never told them where he put it, and twenty acres is a lot of ground.

The symbols of blessing become the track upon which the blessing travels. A check is merely a piece of paper. Even if it is signed by the payee with sufficient funds to cover the stated amount, it is still only a piece of paper until it is delivered to the recipient and deposited in that person's account.

An unspoken blessing is like an uncashed check. The blessing begins a creative process when it is spoken.

God spoke the world into existence. God said, "*Let there be light.*" God said, "*Let there be an expanse between water...*". God said, "*Let the land produce vegetation...*". Each time "*God said,*" the creative process was set in motion and the world as we know it began to take shape.

He spoke words of creation and the earth and what it contains came into existence. Words are the carriers of creation. *"By faith we understand that the universe was formed at God's command, so that what is seen was not made out of what was visible" (Hebrews 11:3).*

When God covenanted with Abraham, He blessed him—Abraham in turn blessed Isaac, Isaac blessed Jacob, and Jacob blessed his twelve sons.

A Blessing Becomes A Blessing Only When It Is Spoken.[1]

Language is the body and soul of communication. It may be praise to God, or conversation with another person. The words that are spoken are words of life or words of destruction. Words are powerful. They are man's primary creative power.

Words have meaning. It may be the cooing of a baby with undefined syllables. It could be talk to a small child, or the harsh shouting of a father to a disobedient son. It might be the words of prayer and adoration to the Lord and Savior, or the words of lovers in sweet communion. Words communicate definite meaning. Someone speaks and someone listens. The consequence depends on the level of *communication.* We understand not just the words one utters, but we can feel that person's heart, his hurt, his dreams, and his highest desires, if we wish to.

This is how God planned it. He created us to communicate with one another. To express our hearts, our minds, and our spirits. He created us to receive information, direction, and blessing. He created us to mold the minds and lives of our children with more information, more direction, and greater blessing with each generation.

David instructs us in Psalm 22:30, 31: *"Posterity will serve him; future generations will be told about the Lord. They will proclaim his righteousness to a people yet unborn—for he has done it.*" Our task is to tell each new generation about the Lord.

The Results Of The Blessing

The Spoken Blessing is interpreted as:

Acceptance - "I am speaking to you of my strong love. You are my child. I accept you for what and who you are."

Fulfillment - "You are worthy of my name, my love, the increase of my lifetime."

Release - "I release you to be what God calls you to be."

Notice this same progression in God's covenant with Abraham, (*Genesis 12:1-3*).

"I will make your name great" —Acceptance

"I will make you into a great nation" —Fulfillment

*"All people on earth will be blessed
through you"* —Release

The same principles were reiterated in Deuteronomy 7:13: *"He will love you and bless you and increase your numbers."*

The Promised Land was not the reward of those who left Egypt. It was the inheritance they gave to their children. But it was a meaningful inheritance because the parents and grandparents had worked and suffered for it. This is the *strength* of "the blessing." Parents give to their children not something worthless, or something they came upon by accident, but the fruit of their labors and the sacrifice of their lives. The inheritance of suffering and labor and love.

I remember so keenly the words of blessing in my life. In growing up in a minister's home we attended church frequently. We would go all day Sunday and then to prayer meeting or Bible study at least two nights a week. We would spend a lot of time praying. That included kneeling—praying—waiting on God, and believing Him for the infilling of the Holy Spirit. It meant believing for jobs, healing, unsaved loved ones, wayward children, alcoholic husbands, and finances, to mention a few.

I must admit I did not always enjoy all of these services. They were long, often boring for a young person, and planned for adults. Yet to this day, I remember them as a tremendous positive influence in my life.

There is one experience I remember above all else. Often during times of prayer I would go over in a corner to kneel. There I could pray, or think, or daydream, or sometimes even go to sleep. More than once I would be in my own little world, until suddenly I would hear the voice of Dad as he moved around the room and prayed for individuals. His voice would rise and fall as he came closer. I knew he would eventually get to me, his youngest child.

Automatically, I would prepare for what I knew was going to happen. I would kneel a little straighter, lift my head, and begin to pray a little more in earnest. And then it would happen! Dad would be directly behind me. I would feel those hands of power rest upon my head and invariably be saturated with words something like this: *"Oh God, bless Dan. fill him with Your Spirit, sanctify him, and keep him by Your power."*

My father had not learned to pray from a prayerbook or by listening to men with PhD's after their names. He had learned to pray out of a sense of his own needs. He had learned to pray out of his love for an omnipotent God. I can hear that prayer as he continued, *"Jesus! Keep this boy clean! I put him in Your hands. Call him to ministry. and God, when he goes into the ministry, bless him with a double portion."*

My dad never said to me that he would be disappointed if I did not go into the ministry. In fact, we never discussed it. He just kept praying God's blessing on me for when I went into the ministry!

As time went by, and I got older, and started thinking about girls and such related things, Dad did not tell me who I should date. But I remember his prayer, and I knew he had God's attention. *"Oh, God,"* he would pray, *"Keep Dan pure and holy. Don't let him put anything into his body that would be impure. Don't let him do anything that would be a reproach to Your name."*

Then He would bless me. He would throw his arms around me and pull me to that giant chest, tears would come to his eyes and he would say, *"I love you, boy."*

Those words of blessing were so powerful. They shot into my soul like a ballistic missile. They carried me to untold heights of faith and confidence. I never doubted for a moment the power and presence of God at those times.

When I was eleven or twelve we lived in Kearney, Nebraska. Several of my friends and I were standing on the heat register that was in the middle aisle of the church. In those cold Nebraska winters, this was invariably where early-comers would gather before the service.

On this particular day an older gentleman walked up to me and said, "What's your name?"

I replied, "Dan LeLaCheur."

He said, "Oh, you are Clarence LeLaCheur's son."

"Yes, I am," I responded.

"You are going to be a preacher, aren't you?"

I stammered a "Well—er—I guess so."

He then took out his wallet and removed a one-dollar bill and handed it to me. He said, "Here, this is the first dollar for your ministry." He then put his hand on my head and prayed a blessing on my life and my future ministry. I will always remember Fred Hornshuh, that venerable old saint of God. His words and blessing have never left me.

Negative Words Become a Curse

How often have you heard parents call their children derogatory names? Names like Fatso, Blockhead, Dummy, are some that come to mind. Words or names spoken in a fit of anger can stay with that person for the rest of their lives.

I was talking about this very thing at a pastors conference. A pastor whom I had known for many years related an incident in his life that took place over 60 years ago, when he was ten years old. He was helping his father build something. His father asked him to hand him the hammer. As he did, it slipped out of his hand and fell on his father's foot. His father shouted, "Damn you, Sam! You will never amount to anything." Even while Sam was relating the incident from so long ago, I could sense the pain it had caused and that he still felt. He said he remembered it as if it had happened yesterday.

How wonderful it would have been if his dad had said, "Sam, please be more careful. You're a good help, and I really appreciate you."

Many times an adult's discomfort becomes a child's cross for life. Never say words to a child that you would not want said to you. It does matter! Words by an adult are often burned into the psychic of a child so deep that the scar is far worse than a physical beating. The child often will spend a lifetime trying to remove the curse placed by a parent saying "stupid" or "damn you" or "idiot."

Make Your Words Count

When you speak to your child, affirm him or her. Every child is made in the image of God. He may be slow, she may not be able to speak clearly or move quickly, but you can bless them with positive powerful building blocks of life—giving words of praise and love.

> *"My son, pay attention to what I say; listen closely to my words. Do not let them out of your sight, keep them within your heart; for they are life to those who find them and health to a man's whole body"* (Proverbs 4:20-22).

Don't just say words of praise once. Practice saying positive things to your child daily. They can be words of blessing, strength, and growth.

"You are so nice, _____ ."

"I love your smile!"

"You did a great job," or, if they didn't *"This is a job that you need to work at; you can be the best, but it takes concentration."*

"I am really proud of you."

"I'm really glad you were born into our family."

"You make a difference to us and to others."

"I love you." (Don't assume they know it.)

"Do you know how much God loves you?"

You get the idea. Praise your child. Build him/her up.

Kathleen McGuire, a licensed psychologist, in her workshops on Positive Discipline from Birth to Three says, "What you put into a child is exactly what you get back."[2]

She says if you reflect to your child, *"Oh, you're so cooperative...You are being so gentle with the kitty...What a good plan, you are really thinking!"* You will get a cooperative, gentle child, confident in his or her ability to think and plan. Reflect to your child, *"You are so stupid...How could you do that?...What a dumb thing to do,"* and you will get a child who feels stupid and ugly with no confidence, sure to fail and behave inappropriately.

The child filled to the brim with admiration in the early years has self-esteem overflowing and therefore is able to give to others. Self-confident, he or she can share the limelight. The child who was not admired spends a lifetime seeking attention, good or bad.

My mother often taught at one of the midweek Bible studies. She recognized that, for my age, I was a good reader. Publicly she would often ask me to "come forward and read the scripture for the lesson tonight." Then she would compliment me on how well I read. I was so proud, and of course I wanted to hear her say how well I did. My reading and my confidence improved dramatically because of her interest and her positive comments.

I am afraid the word "blessing" has been somewhat overused without a sense of the real meaning. We have a tendency to "God bless" everyone and everything, possibly because we cannot think of any other appropriate response. We say it when we shake hands, when we sit at the table and pray before we eat, or when someone sneezes.

Of course, it is all right to bless people, as long as it does not detract from the real significance of the word or action.

The Hebrew word for blessing used in the Old Testament is *berakah*. This was the *"passing on or endowment of the power of God's goodness and favor."* In God's covenant with Abraham, the *berakah* was God's *spoken* blessing.[3] God covenanted with Abraham to make him a great nation and to transmit that divine blessing and power to all generations to come.

Therefore, as we have received the blessing according to Galatians 3:29: *"If you belong to Christ, then you are Abraham's seed and heirs according to the promise,"* we also have the power and responsibility to pass it on to our children.

The Raised Hand

There are various symbols of blessing. The Bible mentions not only blessing by speaking and touching, but also by the raised hand.[4] Priests and pastors still use this gesture in pronouncing benedictions and blessing upon individuals or congregations.

It need not be limited to clergy, of course. Parents and friends can use the same gesture to convey "God go with you and bless you."

Raised hands have always been a symbol of receiving God's blessing while in prayer, or of blessing the Lord in praise. *"I will praise you as long as I live, and in your name I will lift up my hands" (Psalm 63:4).*

The Handshake

The handshake originally had two meanings:[5] the binding of a covenant—the blessing from father to son, as well as a physical act of greeting. The handshake is still one of the most common ways in which we greet others. And even though it is a somewhat formal greeting, it creates a bond of sorts even with a complete stranger.

"Pax Vobis"

The expression "Pax vobis" (peace be with you) used by Jesus when speaking with His disciples is an authoritative formula of blessing.[6] *"While they were still talking about this, Jesus himself stood among them and said to them, 'Peace be with you' (Luke 24:36).* "On the evening of that first day of the week, when the disciples were together, with the doors locked for fear of the Jews, Jesus came and stood among them and said, 'Peace be with you!'" (John 20:19).*

Paul uses it repeatedly in his letters. *"To all in Rome who are loved by God and called to be saints: Grace and peace to you* *from God our Father and from the Lord Jesus Christ" (Romans 1:7). "**And the peace of God, which transcends all understanding, will guard your hearts and your minds in Christ Jesus**" (Philippians 4:7).*

John of Patmos places it at the beginning of the Revelation. *"John, to the seven churches in the province of Asia: **Grace and peace to you from him who is, and who was, and who is to come, and from the seven spirits before his throne**" (Revelation 1:4).*

The church quickly took up this formula, which became a tradition among Christians. The *"Pax vobis"* was by no means intended to be a polite greeting. Rather, it is a blessing that brings to its recipients the messianic peace with all that it implies.

The Spoken Blessing comes as a word of *acceptance:* "I accept you for what and who you are." It comes as a *fullfillment:* "You are worthy of my name, my love, the profit of my lifetime." It comes as a *release:* "I release you to be what God calls you to be."

Chapter Eight

Write It On Their Foreheads
Tell The Stories To Your Children

*I*n her book *Man of Vision, Woman of Prayer* Marilee Dunker, says that her father made a covenant with God that he would take care of all the children of the world if God would take care of his children. She goes on to say that God never makes those kind of agreements. Because of that, she and her sisters had serious problems.[1]

My wife and I have made the commitment to keep the blessing alive in our family. This takes a dedication as strong as anything in life. It is greater than building a strong body, and as time-consuming as getting the highest education. It takes the dedication of a missionary to the most difficult place on this earth. *"But from everlasting to everlasting the Lord's love is with those who fear him, and his righteousness with their children's children- with those who keep his covenant and remember to obey his precepts"* (Ps. 103:17-18).

All the accomplishments of the world cannot equal the reward and satisfaction of knowing that your family has received the covenant blessing of God.

The following truths, if *practiced*, will put into action principles that will assure Christian parents the highest result in raising godly children:

Truth 1: God's Covenant of blessing with Abraham.

"The Lord had said to Abram, 'Leave your country, your people and your father's household and go to the land I will show you. I will make you into a great nation and I will bless you; I will make your name great, and you will be a blessing. I will bless those who bless you, and whoever curses you I will curse; and all peoples on earth will be blessed through you'"(Genesis 12:1-3).

Principle: Keep the Covenant and your family will be blessed.

Truth 2: Christ's redemptive act.

"He redeemed us in order that the blessing given to Abraham might come to the Gentiles through Christ Jesus, so that by faith we might receive the promise of the Spirit" (Galations 3:14).

Principle: All who have faith in Christ are eligible to receive the promised blessing.

Truth 3: Build memorial altars when and where God blesses.

"Each of you is to take up a stone on his shoulder, according to the number of the tribes of the Israelites, to serve as a sign among you. In the future, when your children ask you, 'What do these stones mean?' tell them that the flow of the Jordan was cut off before the ark of the covenant of the Lord. When it crossed the Jordan, the waters of the Jordan were cut off. These stones are to be a memorial to the people of Israel forever" (Joshua 4:5b-7).

Principle: Children need a continual reminder of the blessings that God has provided for the family and the nation.

Truth 4: Joshua and his generation died and the next generation did not know what God had done for Israel.

"Joshua son of Nun, the servant of the Lord, died at the age of a hundred and ten. And they buried him in the land of his inheritance, at Timnath Heres in the hill country of Ephraim, north of Mount Gaash. After that whole generation had been gathered to their fathers, another generation grew up, who knew neither the Lord nor what he had done for Israel" (Judges 2:8-10).

Principle: If you do not tell your children of past blessings, they will soon be serving other gods.

When the biblical truth is known, and the principle is put into living action, parents can raise their children with confidence and genuine success. These principles do work. They are not steps of action designed by a psychologist or a motivational expert. They are principles given by God to a people who desperately needed a bond of unity and the power to survive.

Take the time to teach each Scripture. Meditate on it. Apply the principle to your respective situation. Make it yours. It will come alive for today. Perhaps it will become the passion of your heart, as it has become for me. *It still works.*

The instructions for this to Israel follows on the heels of the *Shema*, this is the phrase recited by the Jews as a confession of faith. *"Hear, O Israel: the Lord your God, the Lord is one" (Deuteronomy 6:4).*

"These commandments that I give you today are to be upon your hearts. Impress them on your children. Talk about them when you sit at home and when you walk along the road, when you lie down and when you get up. Tie them as symbols on your hands and bind them on your foreheads. Write them on the doorframes of your houses and on your gates.

When the Lord your God brings you into the land he swore to your fathers, to Abraham, Isaac and Jacob, to give you—a land with large, flourishing cities you did not build, houses filled with all kinds of good things you did not provide, wells you did not dig, and vineyards and olive groves you did not plant—then when you eat and are satisfied, be careful that you do not forget the Lord, who brought you out of Egypt, out of the land of slavery.

...In the future, when your son asks you, 'What is the meaning of the stipulations, decrees and laws the

Lord our God has commanded you?' tell him: 'We were slaves of Pharaoh in Egypt, but the Lord brought us out of Egypt with a mighty hand. Before our eyes the Lord sent miraculous signs and wonders—great and terrible—upon Egypt and Pharaoh and his whole household. But he brought us out from there to bring us in and give us the land that he promised on oath to our forefathers. The Lord commanded us to obey all these decrees and to fear the Lord our God, so that we might always prosper and be kept alive, as is the case today. And if we are careful to obey all this law before the Lord our God, as he has commanded us, that will be our righteousness" (Deuteronomy 6:6-12, 20-25).

God gave to the fathers of Israel instructions on keeping the Covenant. He then gave them these instructions on passing the blessing of the Covenant from one generation to the next. It was simply by word of mouth: telling the children the history of God's repeated blessings upon their parents and grandparents.

More Than Making Memories

So much is written these days, and said about making memories for your family. If you are like most families, you may think that means taking your family on a much-coveted trip to Hawaii, a vacation to Disneyland, or a fishing trip to the north woods. Perhaps it's going to a professional baseball game to see the million-dollar stars. Indeed, these can be memorable times together. But what do you do when you want your children to grow up with a spiritual heritage? Send them to church? Perhaps shut off their favorite TV program, and get out your grandfather's Bible, and say, "Shut up now, everyone, we are going to read about God and pray."

It is amazing how many children grow up with the idea that anything spiritual must be terribly boring. If forced upon them as a duty, they will learn they must put up with it until "I am old enough to get out of here."

Family time with God should never be dull. In fact, it should happen when you are in the midst of building memories. Family time with God should be right in the middle of the most exciting events of the year. So many Christian families are missing it. We have been programmed from a different era. A time without instant media, rockets, and computers. Why should any child think it very exciting to sit quietly and read the Bible for half an hour?

Don't misunderstand. I am for the Bible. I am for family prayer. But parents who want to impress God upon the hearts of their children must make the relationship what it really is—exciting, lifechanging, and meaningful for their lives today.

Here is a plan that many have found to work today: When you have gathered around the campfire roasting hot dogs and marshmallows, ask your son to pray and thank God for the family. Then take a moment to share how God came into your life, or your parents' lives. Be sure you tell them the difference it has made, the excitement, and the joy it has produced. That it is not always easy, but is always real. Let the "talk time" go as long as the family is really "into it". Share the past blessings of God upon the family at an opportune time. When a son has just landed a ten-inch trout and he is feeling so wonderful and accomplished, try quoting Psalm 24:1. *"The earth is the Lord's, and everything in it, the world, and all who live in it."* This is a time when talk about God's creation would be appropriate.

There are hundreds of opportunities to have a family time with God. Have them in times of excitement, tragedy, fear, anxiety, birth, love, and transition. Weave in the stories of your family, the Red Sea crossings, and the Jerichos you've marched around. These stories will eventually become a part of their lives.

Why did the next generation of Israel begin to serve the Baals? The parents did not tell their children the stories! (Judges 2:10) Why? I suspect they got so busy clearing the land, digging wells, planting crops, and fighting the enemy that they failed to take the time to do as God had said and repeat the stories over and over to their offspring.

Why do we forget? We feel we must make a good living for our family. We must send our children to the university. They must have the proper clothes. We must help them to be acceptable in society. We do not want them to suffer poverty like we did. We hope they never have to cross a Red Sea or eat manna in the wilderness. We do everything we can to make them like everybody else in the neighborhood. And then when they turn out that way, we cannot understand why! Like Israel, they grow up owning the land, but worshiping another god.

Can it be true that the average Christian is secularized as much as the average American? I contend they are, maybe a little more, because so many people became Christians during hard times. They were in poverty or physical need and had no other place to turn. Christ became their hope— then their answer. Then life got better economically, or physically, and they put Christ on a shelf and took down a more acceptable god, forgetting what He had done for them.

We must return with our children to the altars. It is imperative that we tell them time after time about the blessings—in the Scriptures, and in our own families. If we do not pour the victories into their lives, they will never know our most meaningful experiences, and have no reason or desire to follow our Savior.

This is what my parents left their children. We heard the

stories of homesteading in the sandhills of Nebraska. We heard about the hardships of those pioneer days. We heard of great-granddad Elisha who lost his life in a prairie fire. We heard of crops that were lost due to drought and grasshoppers. My brother and I would put on my dad's wrestling togs as he told us of his younger days when he wrestled. He would relate exciting stories of footraces and competing in rodeos.

Then, when he had us captivated with those stories, he shared how his little five-foot mother had prayed that God would call a preacher to the sandhills. After much prayer, God heard her heart's cry and a revival swept through Cherry County, Nebraska. Grandmother took all seven of her children to the Cherry County schoolhouse where meetings were being held. It was here that they all found Christ, and their lives began to change.

Then God sent Rev. T. C. Newby, a preacher with a big Bible and big canvas chart of biblical dispensations. He taught them truths about the Second Ccoming of Christ that they had never heard before.

Dad told us how he was set free from alcohol and smoking. How they were so excited with their newfound hope that they would stay at church until the early hours of morning. He said that as soon as they got home, they would start talking about the next time they could go to church.

I believe that to this day God is still honoring the faith of Grandma Ella—the little pioneer woman whose faith could not be denied. She brought her family to Christ. He met their present needs, and they never stopped talking about it.

I am not an advocate of poverty. I used to hate it. Then I tolerated it. Then little by little I grew to respect it. *Poverty of the flesh may be the strongest advocate there is for the Gospel.* It has brought countless numbers of people to the riches of the Spirit.

So many of my contemporaries became so preoccupied with success. 'Taking the Land', they did not build the altars. They failed to tell their children what God had done to bring them out of poverty. Now the new generation does not have an appreciation for God's blessings. The unhappy fact is that so many of these families are broken by the principles they failed to keep. They are serving other gods.

Satan is often happy to see Christians prosper financially, because at this time he is able to steal their reality. He takes the thoughts of eternity from their minds and replaces them with thoughts of the temporal.

Mardell, my wife, and I used every method that my parents used in passing on the blessing to our children. We shared our experiences of childhood. We recounted the salvation of our parents. Mardell started to Sunday school at a very tender age. It was not long until her parents followed her to church where they soon found Christ. She recounted those stories to our children. She shared about her father's drinking problem, then the change that came into his life upon finding Christ.

Telling the stories is far more than simply telling the stories. These stories and their truth become imbedded into the fiber of our souls. They reach into our minds and our thought patterns. They describe the faith of generations past, and help us develop a faith to live by today.

The stories of God's work in the lives of people we love are so powerful that they become entwined with the daydreams, goals, and successes of a new generation.

This is the power of blessing our children. Sharing our heartbeat with them., as we speak and tell of blessings and battles won, until the past melts into the present, and carries this generation into the future.

One Generation From The Old Rugged Cross

A pastor was looking for a home in a southern city of the country. He and the real estate agent had looked at several homes and were engaged now in light conversation. Off-handedly the real estate man said, "You may have heard of my father?"

"Who was your father?" the pastor asked.

"George Bernard," the man replied. "The man who wrote the hymn '*The Old Rugged Cross*.'"

The pastor said he was pleased to meet the son of such a well-known songwriter. He then asked, "By the way, where do *you* go to church?"

The real estate agent slowly responded, "Well, you know, I have just become so busy since I started selling real estate. Sunday is our busiest day, and I just don't go to church anymore."

The pastor then inquired, "You mean you are not serving the Lord?" The man admitted that he wasn't, he had just gotten too busy. *One generation from the "Old Rugged Cross!"* What happened! Could it be that someone was too busy to keep the faith alive?

We constantly talk to our four grandsons about the blessings of the past in their families. All of them found Christ around the age of four, so we often ask them to tell us how it happened. We ask them to explain as many details as they can remember.

I am convinced if they do not repeat it often they will forget it. How many people have you heard say, "I don't remember when I found Christ. I have just been a Christian all my life." There had to be a starting point somewhere. We do not want our children to forget such a momentous decision by the time they are sixteen! A constant reminder and confirmation of that decision and commitment will instill the most important experience of their life in their minds and hearts, for their whole life.

A friend and I were sharing our testimonies with each other. She shared how one of her children was serving God and the other one was not. She then told me how she had found Christ. Her parents were unsaved, yet she had a marvelous experience of being redeemed by Christ. Tears were flowing freely as we both were touched by her experience. When she was finished, I asked, "Have you ever told your children this story?"

She suddenly had a look of shock on her face as she replied, "No, I never have." I emphatically encouraged her to do so at her earliest opportunity.

I have repeated that question to dozens of people. It always amazes me that so many families fail to tell the ones they love the most important events of their lives. David reflected on this in Psalm 78. Following is my paraphrase:

To my dear family:
As I open my mouth to speak
please listen carefully.
I want to tell you things from past generations.
Those things that our fathers told us.
We must not keep them
from the children of the next generation.
The Lord did wonders and deeds of power.
He laid down the law for Israel
and made statutes that our parents
were to give to the next generation.
They are to be passed from children to children,
even to those yet to be born.

They will put their faith in God,
because they will never forget His deeds.
If this happens, they will not have
the problems of their forefathers;
they were stubborn and rebellious
and disloyal to God.
They failed to keep God's covenant,
and refused to live by His law.
They forgot what He had done,
and the wonders He had shown them.

The principles of blessing your children are as true today as they were when they were given by God to Abraham. The key to blessing was never the physical aspect alone of the material birthright. The power of the familial relationship was the common thread that connected generation to generation.

Both the generational blessing and the generational curse are generated from the same source.

There are three ways in which this can be seen:[2]

1. The *genes* that one inherits from his forefathers never cease to affect one's life.

2. Children learn to become what their parents are by the *example* that is set by their parents, rather than by what they teach.

3. Finally, sin or blessings and their effects descend by the law of *sowing and reaping.*

In the early chapters we saw how a curse could grow and be passed from generation to generation. That curse can be broken by the power of Christ and the steps suggested.

The blessing can likewise be started and passed from generation to generation. It will not be passed by osmosis. It takes a conscious act of blessing. This includes physical touch, and verbally speaking words of acceptance, fullfillment, and release.

There must be a continuity of actions in this relationship. Words never speak louder than actions. Fathers and mothers must seek God often for the grace needed to raise a new generation. *Ephesians 6:4* emphasizes *"Fathers, do not exasperate your children; instead, bring them up in the training and instruction of the Lord."* Continuity of actions can only be equaled by parents' persistence in reminding their children of God's touch upon their lives. This must be done just as one would provide water and sunshine for the growth of a beautiful rose bush. One drink is not enough, one ray of sunshine is insufficient. Daily blessings and daily sharing the past blessings are the keys to sustaining children of any class or any culture.

"One generation will commend your works to another; they will tell of your mighty acts. They will speak of the glorious splendor of your majesty, and I will meditate on your wonderful works. They will tell of the power of your awesome works, and I will proclaim your great deeds. They will celebrate your abundant goodness and joyfully sing of your righteousness" (Psalm 145:4-7).

How To Talk To Your Children

Talk directly—Do not speak indirectly or use words or examples that require guessing about the meaning. There should be no room for misunderstanding.

Do not lecture or preach—Your son or daughter has no doubt heard the sermons. He or she wants to know if you love him or her, and if you approve of them.

Fathers: If you need help in knowing how to open a

conversation with your child, your wife can probably give you a couple of good ideas. Talk to her.

Do it now—Most fathers confess that they plan to talk, but later.

Part Three
Pitfalls

There are numerous pitfalls that the world and Satan present that families can avoid. We must be aware of them and make preparation with our families as to how we will deal with them when they appear in our lives. An overview of some of the pitfalls that most modern families will face is presented here.

Chapter Nine

Pitfalls For The Family
A Warning Label on Some Modern-Day Snares

*S*trict *Religious Faith Lifts Mind As Well As Spirit.*"
This headline in the August 2, 1993 *USA TODAY*
caught my eye. It went on to say, "Followers of 'that old time
religion,' a favorite target of comics, may have the last laugh;
their faith gives them a strong mental edge."[1]

Sheena Sethi of Stanford University, and Martin E. P.
Seligman from the University of Pennsylvania came to this
conclusion after they had separated 623 members of nine
sects into three groups—Fundamentalists, Moderates, and
Liberals. They found that the most optimistic, less likely to

depression, were those with a viable, more literal interpretation of God. The Liberals were far more pessimistic, and the one-third Unitarians who didn't believe in God, were the most pessimistic of all.

Optimism was linked to allowing religion to influence one's daily life—what you eat, what you wear, when you marry, and the eternal hope it gives.

We cannot say that as a Christian family there will never be difficulties or hard times in keeping children safe. The writer of Ephesians 6 gives us several insights into what we will face and how to win. *"Put on the full armor of God so that you can take your stand against the devil's schemes."* He then gives us the armor and the instruments of warfare. There are pitfalls that should put us on guard. Some of these: are part of our heritage; some we cannot avoid. I have found that if we are aware of the dangers of the road, we can travel it with far more confidence. Here are some pitfalls that families will have to deal with in the journey of life.

Religiosity—"excessively, obtrusively, or sentimentally religious."

Religion has been a blessing and a curse for centuries. It has kept whole groups of people aligned to a code of ethics and a pattern of worship. While on the other hand, it has kept much of this group from experiencing deep and personal communion with God. It has substituted ritual for reality in worship and prayer. When religion turns into religiosity it becomes a curse, in that the church or its trappings replace holiness, praise, and a close personal understanding and relationship with God.

I am not talking about liturgy in itself. I am referring more to the mind-set that substitutes an excessive sentimental feeling for the created (buildings, places, things)for the love of the Creator.

Thousands of followers and dabblers in the New Age religion are those from religious homes. There was plenty of religious tradition, and church attendance. Even the reading of scripture, and demonstration of good works. Nevertheless, there was a serious dearth of personal reality and experience. Many people who have left the New Age movement say the reason they got involved was a deep hunger for a personal relationship with God, which they never found in their church. Many admitted to having a longing for spiritual power and significance.

Scores of people in their search for this personal reality in their traditional church have drifted into churches of other denominations, charismatic or independent fellowships. Sad to say, thousands have drifted away from churches to become agnostics and atheists.

The home has abdicated its position as a haven for spiritual safety and power. The church has convinced its members that membership, financial pledges, and church attendance are equal to being a Christian. So many have thought this is all that is necessary. For a few generations that may have worked. A deep commitment to the church did keep many from going astray. But as time went on, the new generation learned little about the significance of the atonement, justification, regeneration, baptism, and discipleship. In essence, the church that many people attend has lost its power.

When new attacks are leveled against the family, the church is not always the bulwark of strength and power in people's lives. Religion in itself is confining and selfish. Without the power of the Holy Spirit it becomes a bondage and is weaker than a social club because the vitality and spiritual resources are nonexistent.

Please understand. I am not anti-church. I love the church. Most of my life has been spent within the church, but

I recognize its deficiency and disempowerment when it exists only as an institution of religion.

When I asked a young man who is now serving the Lord effectively how the church had failed him, this is what he said. The church was:

- Long on rhetoric, short on example.
- Long on judgment, short on acceptance.
- Long on hell fire, short on mercy and grace.
- Long on doing, short on being.
- Long on tradition, short on relevance.
- Long on excuses, short on meaning.
- Long on answers, short on listening.
- Long on program, short on solutions.

Another young man's answer was, "My first thought was that the church did not help me at all, but only damaged me. That probably isn't completely true. I was helped by the church in what I was taught and told. I feel it was a detriment because of what I saw, (i.e., double standards, incredible politics, emotional abandonment, and a judgmental spirit). I never felt accepted in church until adulthood."

In our secularized society, have we allowed dilution of the church so much that our young people are growing up with a bitter taste in their mouths? Families have taken a terrible beating the past twenty years in America. The church must learn how again to be the strength of the individual and the family. Many of those who have left the church in search of other gods, (i.e., materialism, hedonism, or mysticism) will soon find a dead-end. Hopefully, if they come back to the church we will be able to offer them more than religion. *"For we are to God the aroma of Christ among those who are being saved and those who are perishing. To the one we are the smell of death; to the other, the fragrance of life." (2 Cor. 2:15-16).*

Set your family ideals on the person of Christ, not religion. Help each individual to grow and mature with the blessing resting upon them. Character, personality, gifts, and ambition can be positively influenced within the family as parents bless their children and lead them step by step. Mere religion is a stench in the nostrils of God.

Change, Choice, and Political Correctness

Satan has continuously chipped away at the church in America to change its traditional value system. The considered sins of the early 20th century are nearly all accepted values by large numbers of church members in America today. *God's laws have gone from the ten commandments to the ten suggestions to the ten actions a person does if he is not bound by an archaic church with oppressive teachings.*

Change

In 1992 a presidential candidate whose battle-cry of "change" persuaded the American electorate to put him in office. His idea of change was of course mostly political and economical. The elevated place he has given homosexuals, and abortion rights, in a heretofore traditional Christian heterosexual society, indicates that social and religious change are also on the agenda.

Change has often been the theme of new generations, especially those who have not received the blessing from their fathers. This is evident in almost every culture. There is a healthy change that comes with the progress of civilization, and spiritual change that develops with growth. Change in and of itself is necessary and healthy.

Two kinds of change took place during and immediately following the Industrial Revolution. One was the change in working conditions brought about by the many inventions that revolutionized society. The automobile and the telephone not only transformed transportation and communication, but it put millions of people on the work force. The second change was the value system of the American people. Values once based on a relationship with God, began to shift.

Individuals began to boost their egos with material success, rather than relational success. Fathers and sons no longer worked side by side in the fields or as mentor and apprentice. The training of children began to be left up to outsiders—public schools, employers, and those not primarily concerned with personal integrity and God-consciousness. Until World War II, the wife and mother was still at home while dad was working 50 to 80 hours a week. After the war, the women began to join the work force in droves. Then in the 70s and 80s as the Feminine Movement gained power, the home lost its strength, and the divorce rate soared.

Many hidden evils of previous times became the open scourge of changing society—child abuse, sexual abuse, gang warfare, drive-by shootings, murder by children, abortion, and the elevation of the homosexuals. Not least of all were the wholesale adoption of the theory of evolution, values clarification, and the moral dilemma that stems from a lack of spiritual foundation.

The blame for society's condition has been too easily placed with television, an educational system gone astray, and a political system filled with self-serving and dishonesty.

These are the results of the real problem—the breakdown of the home, the often weak relationship of parents and their children, and an impotent church that has by-and-large been unable to give families spiritual stability and moral reinforcement.

The changes that I have summarized briefly here have

left a spiritual void in our present generation. As parents whose desire it is to pass on God's promised blessing to our children, we must re-evaluate where changes can be made that will allow this to happen. One effective way to protect your children from society's pitfalls is to teach them *how to think in spiritual terms*. Not that they become "so heavenly minded that they are no earthly good," but so that they can evaluate the systems of this world in a biblical perspective.

This is learned by children whose parents keep their own values in order. And by parents who share often with their family these values, the reason for them, the results and benefits, and how they apply to daily life. One way to reinforce this concept is to join with another family, with children of similar ages to yours, in times of discussion and learning. Don't be afraid to talk about problems and deal with difficult questions. If we don't do this at home, the television and the school will do it for us—and you can be sure the perspective of each will not be the same as yours.

Choice

Choice—it sounds so twentieth century. So modern. So mature! Why would we want to take choice away from anyone at any time? After all, are we not civilized, educated, and enlightened? Only the Neanderthals from the Stone Age would negate anyone the "right" of choice.

We hear voices telling us: "Let your children have the choice of whether or not to attend church, memorize Scripture, or be a participating member of your family in any endeavor."

"Let them make their own choice concerning premarital sex, (as long as they use a condom)." "Let your sons or daughters choose if they want to work for a living or not. They may want to get on a motorcycle and bike off to Colorado for a year or two!"

"By all means, teach your daughter that she has the choice to have an abortion if she wants to. After all, it is her womb. It doesn't belong to some selfish moralist who does not know what it is like to have a baby."

The word "choice" means far more than pregnant women entering abortion clinics and coming out "unpregnant." It has been made to sound like the "fairness doctrine" of the twentieth century. The word continues to confuse. It changes meaning for the convenience of political and moral purposes. It is not, nor will not be defined as *Webster's Dictionary* states: "A sufficient number and variety to choose from."

Choice, according to definition, ought to mean that a teenager should have the option of carrying a Bible to public school, or stopping in a hallway with a few friends, joining hands, and praying together. Most of all it should mean a teen should have the choice to carry her baby to term, then keep it, or allow it to be adopted by some loving family.

Here is the danger for your children. When Satan and his followers do not like the definition of certain expressions he changes meaningful words to fit his agenda. Words like "gay," changed to mean "sodomy"; "choice" to mean "acceptable abortion"; "love" to be used in the context of "lust."

Teach your children to be aware of the meaning of words. When society begins to take a time-tested word and use it with new meaning, it usually is a cover-up of sin. No matter what sin is called, it is still sin. Sin is rebellion against God. The Bible explains this process. *"For rebellion is like the sin of divination, and arrogance like the evil of idolatry. Because you have rejected the word of the Lord, he has rejected you [as king] (1 Samuel 15:23).*

"The spirit clearly says that in later times some will abandon the faith and follow deceiving spirits and things taught by demons" (1 Timothy 4:1).

The reason young people are trapped into this confluent system of thinking is that it appears to be so understanding or accepting. The basic psychology of a conformable society is that "you ought to accept people as they are—don't you want them to accept you as you are?" But the outcome of such thinking is that nothing is sin anymore—no one needs to repent, because that would make them feel inferior about themselves. Young people who are indoctrinated with a values-clarification system of education will unwittingly fall into this trap.

Lynne, our youngest daughter, was a senior at Valley High School in West Des Moines, Iowa. Her Sociology teacher brought individuals into the classroom to present their viewpoints and philosophy of life. My wife and I were somewhat non-plussed when Lynne came home one day and shared that a young lady who was a masseuse had spoken in class that day. What shook us up most was that her business had come across to the students and the teacher as perfectly legitimate and lucrative, even though she served men and women in a questionable setting. *She simply ran a massage parlor* that fronted for her prostitution. We explained to Lynne that she was probably a prostitute and that being a masseuse was just a high-class French name for it. Nothing we could say made any difference to what Lynne and her friends thought about the young woman, until about three months later when her face was flashed on the television screen with the news story that she had been found dead in the trunk of a car. Choice is a good and beautiful concept when we learn how to make the right choices.

Begin at the earliest moment to define scriptural values—heaven, hell, righteousness, sin, God, Satan, repentance, and forgiveness. Pour these concepts into your children with love and understanding. They will then have less trouble avoiding pitfalls of Satan.

Political Correctness

A new definition of the term *political correctness* says: "To be politically correct is to say those things that make every minority or endangered species feel good about itself or feel valuable." We need to understand that being politically correct is not necessarily a godly concept. For instance, the implication that "a spotted owl ought to have a better chance at living than an unborn baby," is certainly a flawed concept.

On the other hand, some things that are "politically correct" are right and good: "Minorities ought to have the same opportunities to succeed as all other races and cultures." And certainly "Men and women who do equal work should have equal pay."

The danger in being politically correct is to allow others to choose your moral values. Children should be taught values whether they are politically correct or not.

The legalization of abortion, living together outside of marriage, the acceptance of homosexuality as an alternate lifestyle, the distribution of condoms in public schools, all would have been socially and morally unacceptable 30 years ago. Righteousness has been substituted with political correctness. Tolerance is more important than truth. Seventy percent of Americans have been led to believe that there is no absolute truth. Those who quote traditional values, or the Bible, have become the villains.

Therefore, whereas the name "Christian" used to signify honesty, truth, and morality, it has for some become a term of derision. For the liberal media to say one is a Christian is not enough today. Most often they are called "the fanatical religious right," or "the fundamental fringe."

Many people now believe tolerance is more important than truth. They feel that those who believe the words of the

Bible are very intolerant of sin. In the eyes of the politically correct, it is wrong to tell people they are wrong. So when we do not accept someone's actions, we are bigoted, prejudiced, homophobic, and insensitive.

To be a Christian today is about as popular as it was under Nero in Rome. The politically correct would insist that we censor nothing perverse or immoral. Yet they think nothing of censoring the *teachings of Christ and the Bible.*

Recently I spoke at a ministers' seminar, I wanted to show my political correctness, so I opened the session with this greeting: Superintendent Rogers, distinguished ministers, friends; those who are friendly, those not so friendly, friendless. People of height, the vertically constrained. People of hair, those of minimal hair, and those who have guns with hair triggers. The optically challenged, the temporarily sighted, the insightful, the out-of-sight, the out-of-towners. Eurocentrics, the Afrocentrics, the Afrocentrics with Eurorail passes. Staff people, people with staff infection, those with infectuous laughs. Pre-tribulationists, Mid-tribulationists, and those who will be left when the rest of us are gone. Calvinists, Armenians, Russians, Swedes, English, and German Shepherds. Easterners, Southerners, Midwesterners, Midwives, and wives of men going through mid-life crises.

Political correctness comes across with about the same amount of nonsense!

Abortion, A Generational Curse

Abortion—*I wish it was legal and no one wanted to do it.* The reason for that statement is this: We have become a nation of man-made laws. The founding fathers of this nation based most all of their laws upon biblical principles. This can no longer be said. The process by which our system works, by allowing man-made laws to determine morality—what is right or wrong—says abortion is morally right if the Supreme Court wills it so. If, for some reason the Supreme Court changes its collective mind and makes it an offense, then it is morally wrong.

One of the main reasons God instructed the Israelites to take the Promised Land with violence, that is to destroy the people there, was because the people in that land had defiled His creation by sacrificing babies to their gods. God knew that there would intermarriage, and a dilution of their faith in Him. And they soon would be sacrificing their children as the heathen did.(See Deuteronomy 18:9-13.)

Therefore, we answer strictly to man's law. It may come about by popular demand. It may come about because the spirit of the age (led by Satan) captivates the minds of judges, legislators, or presidents.

So because the law says we can kill our baby, it makes it right! How totally foolish. Not just foolish, but stupid! Not just stupid, damnable! Man's law is only worth its justification when it is in compliance with God's law. Therefore, we are deluded into believing that we in this nation only answer to man's laws, and there is no higher law.

When Israel was without a king, *"Everyone did what was right in his own eyes" (Judges 17:5).* Idolatry and misdirection were the order of the day.

Parents, if you are earnest before God, in prayer, seeking His direction, and reading and obeying His Word, you can expect your children to *know* Him, not just *about* Him.

America, long known as the land of freedom is fast carving its destiny of slavery and bondage as it proceeds down this path of moral decay and destruction. I hesitate to speculate on the consequences of abortion. If AIDS has come about because of sexual sin, what will the natural consequences of sacrificing our children be?

God is sovereign. He will do as He wills. He has given this world His Word, and many are not ignorant concerning His plan. We must teach His principles to our children.

Many women whom I have talked with were convinced an abortion would solve their immediate problem, but found that, instead, it left them with:

- A deep hurt.
- A guilt that would not go away.
- An anger that festers like a sliver under a fingernail.
- A loss of dignity.
- A loss of the sense of the sacredness of life.
- A loneliness comparable to that of a mother who loses a small child.
- A callousness of spirit.

Experience and common knowledge tells us that Christian girls get pregnant too. We cannot stick our heads in the sand about this issue. We must be prepared to deal with this eventuality in a loving manner.

What do you tell your pregnant unmarried daughter?

- We love you. We are sorry that you did not wait until you were married to have a baby.
- We will stand by you every step of the way in the delivery of this child.
- Our wish is that you do not have an abortion. We believe that this goes against God's principle of life.
- We will do everything we can to help you raise this child. We will stand with you if you decide that you cannot keep the baby and wish to give it up for adoption to a fine Christian family.
- Now let us pray and ask God for forgiveness and His blessing.

Where Does Aids Fit In?

Is AIDS a curse from God? When one begins with the premise that the breaking of natural laws leaves mankind susceptible to natural judgments, it is.

In the list of God's don'ts, He said, *"Thou shalt not commit adultery."* Contingent upon broken commanments, there has always been a perceived and felt punishment.

Today, since we are living under grace, we commonly think that God will overlook broken covenants. It appears that occasionally individuals are immune to God's punishment, in relation to broken moral laws. God often allows the results of sin to accumulate, generation upon generation. Then suddenly the consequences are so evident that only sin-blinded mankind cannot comprehend them. *"Those of you who are left will waste away in the lands of their enemies because of their sins; also because of their fathers' sins"* (Leviticus 26:39).

Dr. Les Breitman, a completed Jewish Doctor in Denver, says this about AIDS.[2]

Is it possible that God is sending a message of judgment by this plague called AIDS? Let us look to some medical history—in conjunction with God's Word. Long ago, God instructed man not to fornicate. A man and a woman were to leave their parents and be bonded to each other as one flesh in holy matrimony. Sex outside of those holy vows, taken before God, is deemed by God himself to be fornication.

But man, nevertheless, fornicated. As a result, man has contracted gonorrhea, syphilis, yaws, chancroid, lymphogranuloma venereum, granuloma inguinale, to name a few venereal diseases. (Beg pardon! Today we must be politically correct and call them sexually transmitted diseases—or better yet, STD's. Sounds better!) Were these diseases spawned of judgments sent from God for violating His commandment concerning fornication? Would anyone deny that these diseases could not have existed if man had obeyed God and not fornicated?

But our loving God permitted man to find cures for these diseases borne of mans's failure to obey God. He permitted man to discover antibiotics to fight these diseases. But instead of: thanking God and obeying Him, man could now fornicate without fear of dying of venereal disease. While man was discovering these antibiotics, and also discovering that he could fornicate without fear of dying, science also developed pills that would allow him to fornicate without fear of pregnancy.

The arrival of artificial birth control methods on the scene of man's fornication was followed shortly by the advent of a new disease: genital herpes. Oh, the herpes virus had been known to physicians for quite some time, but it had never been a problem to man; it had never before been infectious. But now with the advent of "free" sex occasioned by the "pill," herpes became a national scourge, infecting both men and women and being transmitted by them from one to another. Herpes was forever; there was no cure; it was recurrent, popping up a day or so after sexual stimulation in a substantial portion of the sexually active population. It has become the second most frequently transmitted sexual disease. Strangely, genital herpes did not significantly trouble the married population—those that entered holy matrimony instead of fornicating.

Protected by the marriage vows they took before God? I wonder."

No antibiotic has ever been developed that is definitively curative of herpes. It has been learned that herpes, in addition to being recurrent for life, has a tendency to be carcinogenic, associated with cancer of the cervix in the female, of the prostate in the male, and of the bladder in both sexes, depending upon which authority is read.

But did man yet learn not to fornicate, even when faced with the dreaded results of such disobedience to God? No, he not only continued to fornicate, but he also encouraged the homosexual community to come out of the closest and to practice their unhygienic sexual disobedience to God's commandments with no further threat of punishment from their fellow man. Well, if man refuses to punish according to God's commandments, it seems that God steps in with His own judgments against mankind. Isn't that the way it was throughout the Old Testament? The Israelites sinned, and God punished.

The virus that causes AIDS is a new creation. If it were here among men in times past, we would certainly have known about it, because it is the greatest scourge upon mankind that has ever been visited on the earth. It is ultimately fatal 100% of the time, and it cannot be destroyed by any agent presently known to man. The bubonic plague (Black Plague) pales by comparison.

Some will claim that the virus has indeed been present since times of old, but that it has never affected man until now. Such a theory requires a real stretch of the imagination. that such a virulent and hardy organism could remain dormant and hidden for so long. If this was true—that the AIDS-causing virus had been on earth for an indefinitely long period of time— then we should consider why it suddenly emerged when mankind now rebels again against God's command- ment that man should not lie with another man. This is reminiscent of God's wrath as described in the Book of Revelation, where, upon the pouring out of the vial by the sixth angel, three evil spirits appearing like frogs come out and perform miraculous, but evil, signs— such as AIDS. It is also reminiscent of the demons and the four horsemen of the apocalypse who are held in abeyance until the time of the end, when God calls them forth to plaque mankind. Is AIDS the forerunner of this type of judgment? I again wonder.

Will there be a cure for AIDS?

The only possible answer is: **If God wills.**

Dr. Breitman explained that with our present knowledge there can be no cure for a long time, maybe never. Cure can come only with a miraculous breakthrough in medicine. We know it has happened before with polio and diphtheria.

If the fight against AIDS is dependent upon medical science's present state of knowledge, then there can be no cure. With all of science's past conquest in the area of curing dread diseases such as polio, small pox, and diphtheria, to name just a few, the medical scientist had to first determine which pathogenic microorganism was causing the disease. He was then required to test various chemicals and other agents to discover which ones would kill the disease-causing organism without injuring or killing the human host. Sometimes this process required the researcher to actually develop new types of antibiotics to be tested on the new disease.

Until now, medical science has always risen to this challenge, even though trial and error sometimes required extended lengths of time before success could be achieved. But as a result of the unusual attributes of the AIDS virus, we face an absolutely insurmountable task. Because this particular virus mutates so often, whatever antimicrobial agent we employ to poison the virus fails very soon. Whenever the virus comes into contact with a noxious element, it simply changes its own makeup so as not to be adversely affected by that harmful agent. In other words, the virus possesses a perfect defense mechanism. We have never before faced a microorganism with this capability. If such a microorganism had been in existence before, medical science certainly would have known about it, because it would have survived even until today.

A cure for AIDS can therefore come to us only by virtue of a miraculous breakthrough in the concept of fighting disease. That means that a cure can come only through a miraculous intervention of GOD. Man has absolutely no experience with this type of problematical mutating virus, and so he cannot succeed alone in vanquishing this foe! He needs a miracle. *Will God provide such a miracle?*

My heart's prayer is that a cure is found, but certainly not to allow mankind to sin against their bodies and against God. Christians need to pray that like most of the plagues of history, we will learn the lesson God intends.

Sex education begins in the home. Parents must not only talk about the "facts of life" but must teach their children openly and honestly. Teach the sacredness, the blessedness, the joy of sex in marriage. Teach the devastation of premarital sex, extramarital sex, and the homosexual lie.[3] We are at the place in our society where we can no longer treat this subject as a taboo in our homes. A moral and physical plague is sweeping the world. The cure will come through families who are willing to face the issues. Hold up biblical values and *pass on the blessing.*

We know that these terrible diseases affect many who are completely innocent. There are other ways of contracting AIDS than by sexual means. Sin always affects the community and the nation: "The rain falls on the just as well as the unjust" (Matthew 5:45)KJV. It is the responsibility of spiritual leaders, and national leaders to warn the people of sin and its results.

Do not allow the world, television or, public schools to educate your sons and daughters with immoral values. Start now. Get a battle plan! Work together as a family, or with other families. *The curse of past generations can be broken. Generational blessing can begin with this generation.*

---

[3] Turn to ENDNOTES to read what Dr. Breitman has to say about homosexuality.

Environment
Animal Rights
Spotted Owl
Sierra Club
Greenpeace

Psychology
Human Potential
Mind Power
Parapsychology

Holistic Healing
Reflexology
Acupunture
Psychic Healing
Homeapothy
Vegetarianism

Entertainment
Movies
TV
Music
Stars

**New Age
in the
Marketplace**

Education
Evolution
Values Clarification
Centering
Guided Imagery
Visualization
Outcome Based Ed.

Games
Dungeons & Dragons
Ouija Boards
Masters
He Man

Drugs & Alcohol
Tune In
Turn On
Tune Out
Sacraments of the
New Age

Meditation
TM
Yoga

What is practiced in the marketplace
soon becomes the religion of the people.

Chapter Ten

More Pitfalls
Gods Of The New Age

It all sounds so good. Listen to the music:
    Turn your fears into hopes.
    Learn to relax.
    Lose weight — stop smoking.
    Find the ultimate answer for your love life.

Then the music changes keys, and you hear,
    How to get in touch with your real self.

How to turn on the power of the universe to capture your desires.

Power over others — in selling, in speaking, in love.

Learn from the ancients the secrets of life.

Again the music shifts into a faster beat, the volume increases, and the message becomes deadly.

You are actually God.

There is no other power higher than you.

Live good in this life, and be reborn to a higher existence.

You shall never die.

The direct assault upon the family by New Age voices is so insidious, so diverse, yet so contrary to biblical truth. Marilyn Fergeson, the high priestess of the New Age culture says in her book, *The Aquarian Conspiracy*[1], that a paradigm shift must take place (when a consensus of understanding or belief in any field goes through radical change) in our society. We have watched this paradigm shift take place in the intervening years. The conduct that we considered wrong 30 years ago has become the norm today. Actions that were good and wholesome have been cast aside as obsolete and undesirable.

Twenty-five years ago a group of drug-induced hippies spoke in mystical tones about creating a new age. Most of us thought they were kooks living in a dream world on the fringes of society.

"Woe to those who call evil good and good evil, who put darkness for light and light for darkness, who put bitter for sweet and sweet for bitter" (Isaiah 5:20).

Let us look at some of the places that our children will be tested as they mature.

Education

I am convinced that the battle for mankind's future is now being waged and won in the public school classrooms by teachers who perceive their role as the proselytizers of a new faith.

"The classroom must and will become an arena of conflict between the old and the new — the rotting corpse of Christianity, together with all its adjacent evils and misery, and the new faith. . . resplendent in its promises. . ." (John Dumphy, "*The Humanist*"[2])

All public education is not New Age, nor is it all bad. There are many wonderful dedicated teachers in the public educational system. On the other hand, public schools have become a hotbed of New Age teaching. The flower power of the 60s and 70s has bloomed in the 80s and 90s. Those who have gone into education with the hippie and peacenik mentality have carried over much of their beginnings to a more spiritual and deadly world view.

Philosophy and religion classes in Universities from Berkeley to Boston became breeding grounds for this ideal.

In helping you understand the difference in Christianity and the New Age doctrine is, here is a comparison of both views:

Christianity	New Age
God	
God is personal.	God is impersonal.
God is separate from His creation.	"It" is one with creation.
God creates by the power of His Word and sustains the creation.	It is eternal and eternally changes its forms.

Christianity	New Age
God	
God is the same at all times.	God is change.
Mankind	
Humans are personal.	There is an illusion of individuality.
Humans are fallen and sinful.	Humans are ignorant victims of illusion.
The remedy is moral regeneration by means of the Cross.	The remedy is knowledge of ones' true nature.
Humans are limited and finite.	Humans have infinite potential.
Humans are answerable to God.	Humanity is answerable to no one.
Humans are to pursue good and avoid evil.	Humanity must transcend categories of good and evil.
Redeemed human reason can be trusted to discern many truths; intuition is sometimes reliable also.	Reason is illusion, intuition, based on "all is one," apprehends truth.
Creation	
Similarity of forms, diversity of nature	All is one; you, me, (a carrot) and the whole universe.
Nature and the universe are created, finite, and subordinate to humans; created in the image of God.	Nature is unlimited and can be of greater, equal, or sometimes less important than humans.
Only God is to be worshiped	Anything and everything can be worshiped.

Christianity	New Age

Creation

Christianity	New Age
Change and renewal come by God's providence and direct influence.	Non-personal forces of organic and spiritual evolution account for change.
Adaptation and development are intelligent designs.	

Adapted from a chart by Richard Beswick[3]

The ultimate goal of New Agers is to complete the change of consciousness, or the paradigm shift. As we look at eight areas of New Age influence in our world we must come to the conclusion that the shift has about been completed.

Several years ago my wife and I received a call to our radio call-in program from a parent in a suburb of Des Moines, Iowa. She asked if we knew what was happening in a particular elementary school with a program called Kiddie QR. Immediately following the program, I called the school and asked if I could sit in on a second-grade class that was being taught this new idea. I was given permission, and the next morning I walked into one of the strangest situations I had ever witnessed. I found 25 second graders lying quietly on the floor. Since it was too early for nap time, and I knew it was not a tornado drill, I was interested to say the least. I got my first basic education in Quieting Reflexes (Kiddie QR).

The guest teacher began to tell the children that light would begin to pour into their bodies through their eyes, ears, nose and mouth. In fact she stated, "At this very moment you are perfect." Later, as I considered her words, I realized that if they were perfect why would they ever need to submit to a Savior? These innocent children were being brainwashed with anti-Christian, New Age religious teaching.

The teacher went on to name little helpers whom they could call upon in their daily lives, whenever they felt the need. She gave them "fighty fist" to call upon when they were angry.

I was incredulous with my limited knowledge of the New Age nuances, but I realized I had just watched a simplified version of Transcendental Meditation. I had witnessed this channeler give spirit guides (helpers) to a whole class of innocent children.

Later I found out that this kind of activity was prevalent all across the country. It came with a dozen different labels such as self-actualization, magic teacher, success imagery, confluent education, centering, visualization, holistic approach, Holism, and many more.

Most of the time the instructors do not call them "spirit guides." Beverly Galyean, creator of confluent education, who was able to place this in the Los Angeles public schools with federal funds, says that it is a little too obvious, so she calls them "imaginary guides."

Marilyn Fergeson, (*Aquarian Conspiracy*, p. 20) says "of the Aquarian conspirators surveyed, more were involved in education than in any other single category of work. They were teachers, administrators, policymakers, and educational psychologists[4]." Their agenda is to develop the language so it does not sound religious.

One of the textbooks used in Eugene, Oregon, on Guided Imagery and Visualization is *Meditating with Children*. It contains the art of Concentration and Centering by Deborah Rozman. If there was ever any doubt that a religion was being taught in public schools, one only need note to whom the book is dedicated: Paramahansa Yogananda, a Hindu Guru, and to the "One." This is a designation for Brahman, the ultimate reality of Hinduism.

One other experience introduced at Eugene Edison

Elementary School was most interesting. At Halloween, children were instructed to make paper mache' masks of animistic spirits, then write a role play. They were encouraged to identify with the spirit of their mask, what it thought, felt, and did.[5]

New Age visualization techniques are identical to those used by spiritualists to contact demons. Children and the unwary often end up suffering much more than any human power can help them remove. In addition to the possibility of occult bondage, children face a subtle challenge to their faith. If they are taught that their God-given imagination can produce the reality they desire, why follow Christ?

In one case, after a Quieting Reflex session, a little girl refused to pray in the name of Jesus. When asked "Why?" She said her imaginary wise person (or spirit guide) had directed her not to.

> *"The coming of the lawless one will be in accordance with the work of Satan displayed in all kinds of counterfeit miracles, signs and wonders, and in every sort of evil that deceives those who perish. They perish because they refused to love the truth and so be saved. For this reason God sends them a powerful delusion so that they will believe the lie and so that all will be condemned who have not believed the truth but have delighted in wickedness" (2 Thess. 2: 9-12).*

We must take back our public schools. Parents must become involved in school affairs, and in helping choose and direct their children's education. If you cannot change your public school, home-schooling is a viable option. Many Christian parents have found it to be both rewarding to their children and to themselves.

Out-come Based Education

Outcome-based education says, "It doesn't matter what answers a student gives as long as he is trying." The new educator says bad grades only discourage underachievers. This theory gives a subtle message. It says, "You don't have to stretch because it dosn't matter. You won't get a failing grade."

Frankly, this is already too prevelant in our society. I am convinced that the people who have really accomplished great things are those who overcome failure. They studied hard, worked long hours, and invested everything to succeed. Incentives are wonderful motivators for success. Children should be taught that the harder they work the greater the result. Outcome-based education teaches students it is all right to fail as long as you feel good about yourself.

College:

If you knew a vicious pit bull was just across that beautiful lawn, waiting for a tender college freshman to set foot on the sidewalk, would you send your unguarded, unsuspecting young man or young woman across that line? Many secular higher learning institutions are filled with "pit bulls" waiting to devour innocent and naive Christian young people.

Christian parents typically say, "I want Johnny to be a doctor, or an engineer, or a C.P.A.," so off they go to the state university. Some make it spiritually in these institutions, but many do not. I have watched many drop out of church, but even worse seen them lose the foothold they needed so desperately to live in a secular world. I have talked to many whose faith was damaged in college and university. The cities of our nation are filled with educated people whose souls are spiritually dead.

"But if anyone causes one of these little ones who believe in me to sin, it would be better for him to have a large millstone hung around his neck and to be drowned in the depths of the sea" (Matt. 18:6).

What can do we do?

First, we must educate our children. I am 100 percent for education. The process is what I question. Send your sons and daughters to a Christian college. Send them to a Bible college for a couple of years until they are solidly grounded and mature. Then, when they are ready to face the "pit bulls," let them go with spiritual strength, and biblical understanding. There is no education worth sacrificing the souls of our youth. Send them with your love and your blessing. Our young people are the richest resource of the home and church.

Entertainment

"Television is first and foremost an educational medium. It is an instrument of persuasion, indoctrination, seduction, propaganda, and mind manipulation. All done in an entertaining way" (Marlin Maddoux).

Other experts say that TV is strictly existant to make money. Everything is produced for commercial purposes.

Thirty years ago most children grew up in a neo-pagan culture. Today's Saturday morning cartoons on television are filled with religious propaganda. There is much Eastern thought contained in them, from Hinduism, Zen, and Buddism. We must be aware that our children are being indoctrinated with a religion that is the opposite of Christianity, even anti-Christian. Much of this religion has to do with the issue of power: What is it? Who has it? How does one get it? How does it work?

This theme permeates children's programming. The power displayed has a spiritual source, and a supernatural image. It is a force, and an entity beyond the person. It possesses and controls. Most Eastern Religions claim that spiritual power lies within one's own life. It is this force that compels one toward some type of self-realization or self-actualization.[6]

Christians believe that they receive their power through Christ.

Movies, television, music, and most means of entertainment have gone so hi-tech that they are incredible in their presentations. The fascination with technology has caused many Christians to overlook the message that is coming through the medium.

The message is a continual violent, sexual, anti-establishment theme. Its goal is to demean sacred Christian ethics and traditional values. The message is thrust at our families dozens of times daily. Movies, television, magazines, political and economic agendas, all are saturated with the same recurrent melody. It accumulates—layer upon layer, day after day. The indoctrination and seduction never let up. Your children are being brainwashed; at the least neutralized, at the most demonized.

It is not a new problem. Satan has always used the most attractive means of destroying families and homes. *"There is a way that seems right to a man, but in the end it leads to death"* (Proverbs 16:25)

The future looks like more of the same, but with greater scientific help. We are being prepared for the step up in television quality and programming. On the horizon and coming soon is *very high-density television* (VHDTV) with extremely sharp images that are much more realistic. *Holographic television,* with three-dimensional figures, will jump right out of the TV set. *Virtual reality* will allow a viewer to become a participant in broadcast situations. *Fiber optic cable networks* with mini satellite dishes will bring 200 channels into your home. These channels will carry every conceivable idea, philosophy, and spirit—right into your living room.

What Can Parents Do To Counteract This Technology?

- Put time limits on TV
- Know the programs your child views.
- Let your preschooler watch only 30 minutes a day, for example.
- Tape good programs and play them later
- Plan ahead
- Have family members pick their programs in advance
- When a program is positive—reinforce its principles
- When programming is negative (too much excess) stop it and talk about it

Environment

We need to protect our environment from certain abuses. Cruelty to animals is certainly not humane or Christian, but keeping these issues in the proper perspective is important. There is so much publicity about saving the environment that we must not fall into the trap of those who worship the creation rather than the Creator! The spotted owl, the whale, and the snail darter are admittedly issues of our time. When listening to the proponents of animal rights, or environmental issues, be sure to determine their values. Many of these individuals believe in reincarnation, and their big concern is that the spirits of past generations are living within that animal or protected species.

We need to talk about these issues with our families. Make certain your children understand the difference between conservation and stewardship of God's creation, and reincarnation and the worship of nature.

I like the statement I heard about the difference between a Christian and a New Age environmentalist. The New Ager will approach a tree and fall down and worship it. The Christian will thank God for the tree, take his chain saw, cut it down, and build a place of shelter for his family.

Psychology

One of the biggest lies and misnomers foisted upon ambitious individualism is that a person can do whatever his or her mind can conceive. I believe that this is an *untruth* whether used by motivational speakers or healing and faith evangelists. The only person this is true about is Jesus Christ. He is the Son of God. There were no dimensions of time, space, or material with Him. We are not divine. We are mortal, and the limitations of mortality will be with us until we receive a glorified or heavenly body.

Both the New Age guru and the over zealous non-scriptural preacher try to motivate individuals to reach out by faith and receive anything and everything they ask for. The suggestion Satan made to Adam and Eve was:

"Eat of the tree of knowledge of good and evil and you will be as gods." He went on to tell them *"They would never die."* This was an evil ploy to convince them to yield to his plans.

It was a lie, and today remains the deception of the New Age. This is the deceit of reincarnation or transmigration of the soul. The disturbing news is that much of this has crept into our churches. I have heard some modern prophets and prophetesses speak about one's soul traveling through space. The concept that this lifetime is one in a series of incarnations comes directly from Hindu teachings. The idea of reincarnation is deadly. It is *false!* It proposes that one can earn their way to Nirvana (heaven) by gradually working off sins through successive life cycles. It eliminates the whole fact of Christ dying for our sins, and the necessity of our receiving salvation by faith. The Scripture says, *"It is appointed unto men once to die...."*

When psychology is used to employ spiritual gimmickry or to bring about a false sense of power, it is a reprehensible shame.

Biblical truth in its purest form is very exciting and liberating when applied to dull, sin-cursed lives. "Over-the-edge" religion leads to occultic experiences that open one to false doctrine and spiritual danger.

Give your children a balance of biblical facts applied in the reality of practical, everyday experiences.

Games

Startling and powerful weapons in the spiritual battle used against families today are games. Young people have been caught in this treacherous web of deceit. Estrangement from family and church, and even death, have been the result of such games as Dungeons and Dragons and Masters of the Universe. These fantasy role-playing games are dangerous and should be labeled with a skull and crossbones, and marked "may be dangerous to your health."[7]

Parents should know what their children are doing, what they are watching on TV, and what games they are playing. The days are past in which we can allow our children to run free through our neighborhoods and play and do as they please. There are too many moral contaminates flowing through the sewers of godlessness and political correctness.

Be on guard!

Holistic Healing

Holistic Healing is a tenuous practice because there is so much good received from natural methods. Like so many good practices, Satan will infiltrate with his spiritual devices.

Many of the practices listed on the chart on page 137 are not evil in themselves. The danger is that they so often are only one part of the whole. The whole becomes a substitute for faith in Jesus Christ as Redeemer and Healer and Lord of our lives.

Many of those who practice Holistic Healing or are patients of it are New Agers. A valid experience has been used to bring about New Age results.

Be on guard!

Drugs And Alcohol

Here are some suggestions to consider.

When your son or daughter is young, begin an educational process. Teach them not only the inherent dangers of drugs, alcohol, and tobacco, but also the dangers of following the crowd, submitting to peer pressure in such things.

1. Expose your children to all of the anti-drug programs that seem necessary (i.e., films and seminars on the dangers of usage).

2. Expose them to the reality of mouth and lung cancer, emphezema, the devastation of mind-control drugs, and the loss of life and limb due to drinking and driving, etc.

3. Initiate parties in which no alcohol is served.

Peer pressure is the hallmark of drug and alcohol use among children.

There must be an adequate background laid from very early childhood concerning choices, friends, practices.

Families working together in a church or small community can guide their children through these pitfalls.

Meditation

I recently discovered that Yoga was being taught in a Christian church! As I perused a booklet that was being used as a guide, I saw pictures of small children in the position of a cobra. The tenth step of Yoga is to place oneself in the position of a cobra. In actuality it is the invitation to invite Satan into one's body.

Yoga is far more than a method of relaxation. Eastern meditation involves the complete emptying of one's mind of all thought. The power of the universe is then supposed to inhabit the one in deep meditation. What an opportune moment for Satan to enter. He often does, and then individuals are led or inhabited by Satan.[8]

Scores of seekers of peace have become entrapped by becoming involved in some form of TM (transcendental meditation) or Yoga. These classes are taught in YMCA's, hospitals, churches, and schools. Let me emphasize strongly that they are extremely dangerous.

I remember an experience I had while I was lecturing on the dangers of New Age strategy. I had just completed explaining the steps to a "change of consciousness" that is the goal of New Age teachers. I shared how the idea is to knock out the mind so that the will can surrender.[9]

Suddenly, a woman in the group got up from her chair, went to the back of the room and began sobbing. I stopped speaking and asked her if there was something wrong. She said, "You are absolutely right. I was looking for a spiritual high, a power that I had never found. I got into Meditation. I experienced all those beautiful feelings that you mentioned as characteristics of the altered state of consciousness. Then I started going down the other side. I could not take the depression any longer. I got in my car, drove down the street and crashed head-on into a tree, trying to take my life. The reason I am here today is to find the real answer for the lies that I was told."

Transcendental Meditation and Yoga are serious and dangerous practices. Warn your children early about them, long before they become interested or initiated into dabbling with them.

Know your children and their friends. Be strong spiritual leaders. Spend time with your children. No job, no amount of money, status, or pleasure is worth sacrificing this generation. Raising children is fun, frightening, and fantastic. We as parents hold the power of future generations in our hands. Do not let Satan make you lose your grip.

A Biblical Example

Exodus 10:8-9 *"Then Moses and Aaron were brought back to Pharaoh. 'Go worship the Lord your God,' he said. "But just who will be going?" Moses answered, "We will go with our young and old, with our sons and daughters and with our flocks and herds, because we are to celebrate a festival to the Lord."*

The reason they wanted to take their children with them was because they were going to *"hold a feast unto the Lord."* Modern man would say, "What can these little ones possible understand about a feast unto the Lord?" "We don't want to force our religion upon them; after all, when they grow up they can make their own decisions about worshiping God."

Moses and Aaron had no plan of seeking one thing for themselves and another for their children. They did not dream of Canaan for themselves, and Egypt for their children. How could they eat the manna of the wilderness, or the old corn of the land, while their children were feeding upon leeks, onions, and the garlic of Egypt?

Moses and Aaron knew that God's call to them was a call to their whole family. They knew that if the whole family didn't leave Egypt, no sooner would they have left by one road than their children would draw them back by another.

Satan loves to divide families both physically and spiritually. Pharoah knew what division would do. *"Go now, ye that are men."* He knew the brokenness of a divided family and the anxiety it would cause. So many parents are going forth to serve God, but they have left their little ones in Egypt.

The analogy here only deals with the principle. It is true we cannot take our children to heaven as the Israelites took theirs to Canaan. God alone can fashion our children for heaven, by implanting in them the spirit of His own Son. But we can train them for heaven. It is not merely our duty, but our high and holy privilege to do so.

Too many parents bemoan the fact that their children have grown up in church but then do not continue serving God. This is a paradox! We take them to church; they learn to sing the hymns and choruses; they listen to the prayers, and hear the principles that are taught. But throughout the next six days what they learn in scshool and from their peers contradicts all of this. Our little ones are trained by and for the world, unless we intervene. The scope, aim, object, and entire character of their education is worldly in the truest and strictest sense.

The pitfalls have always been there. God's promise to bless our families is just as pertinant today as it was to Abraham, but we must teach them the truths of God's Word, relate the stories of our salvation, and demonstrate the character of faith in their presence. The pitfalls can then be used as building blocks for blessing.

Part Four

Father—The Man He Was Meant To Be

This chapter is directed primarily to fathers but the message is also for mothers. Men are missing the mark of who they are and what their role is in the lives of their wife and children. Fathers must guide their sons and daughters through boyhood and girlhood to manhood and womanhood. An initiation process for the "rite of passage" is here presented and strongly recommended.

Chapter Eleven

From Boy To Manhood
What Kind of Men Are Our Boys Becoming?

*I*n dozens of cultures all over the world there are initiation rites held for the passage of boys into manhood. In tribal societies the experience begins with two events. The first is a clean break from his parents, after which the novice goes to the forest, desert or wilderness to learn how to be a man. The second is a wound that the older men give the boy. This could be the scarring of the skin, a cut with a knife, a brushing with nettles, or a tooth knocked out.

These wounds are not given in a sadistic manner. Those who administer them in most cultures try to insure that the injury does not lead to unnecessary pain. Rather, the infliction reverberates from a rich center of meaning.

An initiatory experience of the Australian aborigines is a good example.[1] The older men of the community take the young boys who are to be initiated into the men's world, away from home. Here they tell them of the first man, Darwella. The boys listen intently to this story of the original man, their Adam.

Darwella is supposedly sitting in a nearby tree. While the young men try to see Darwella in the tree, an old man comes down the line and knocks a tooth from each boy's mouth.

The old men then remind the boys that a similar experience happened to Darwella. He also lost a tooth. For the rest of their lives their tongues associate the broken tooth with a living connection to Darwella. This is a physical connecting link to their origin and to all generations in between. Most of us would give up a tooth for a living connection to Adam. The truth is, we have one in the person of Jesus Christ. He becomes that link in our lives with the first man who took us into sin. He provides a means of forgiveness from all sin. He has broken the curse of sin that we might see the curse of sin broken from past generations.

This story serves as an analogy, in spite of the fact that it comes from those whom we would consider heathen. It is repeated in similar ways in many cultures of the world. Some initiation procedures in the United States could be considered just as heathenistic.

A man named George came to me following a session in which I spoke on this subject. I had said that "In America, we usually don't have initiation ceremonies where fathers take their sons from boyhood to manhood."

George said, "You are incorrect. It happened to me on my sixteenth birthday. My father told me he was going to make a man of me now that I was sixteen." George went on then to explain to me that the initiation was done in two stages. "The first night on my sixteenth birthday, we went to his favorite bar, where he spent a great amount of time with his buddies. He kept ordering drinks for me and made me consume them until I could no longer see or walk. I became insanely drunk and violently ill. I will always remember my initiation into manhood. It was the beginning of what I thought every man did: drink until you become stinking drunk."

A week later when he had sufficiently recovered from the hangover, George's father told him there was a second stage to becoming a man. George related hesitantly, "My dad and I got in his car and drove down to a seamy part of town." He said, "I remember how scared I was as he picked up two women off the street. We then went to a run-down motel and my father initiated me into manhood through an experience with my first prostitute." George went on to tell me that this of course was not his last experience with the ladies of the streets. So you see, we do have heathenistic initiation ceremonies in this country of taking young boys into manhood.

I am convinced that the people of the Old Testament not only knew the power of a generation upon the succeeding generation, but they were specifically involved in a direct initiation process of taking a boy into manhood.

Somewhere in our busy, modern post-Christian era there is a missing link in the relationship between fathers and sons. This missing link is often obvious in young men's lives and is perpetuated with each succeeding generation. Perhaps what is presented in this chapter will help some to restore the missing link in the relationships between sons and their fathers.

Intimacy

When Adam and Eve were still sinless they stood before God—vulnerable, transparent, and without guilt or fear. It was only after they had sinned that they tried to hide from God their nakedness and shame.

Before they fell, these two individuals—man and woman—stood naked before each other without shame, *Genesis 2:25*. Intimacy was possible when they were free to be themselves without the need to play deceptive games.

Shame results in the feeling that one should hide oneself. When shame is present, family members put on masks and play deceptive roles before one another as if they were an audience rather than fellow loved ones. Intimacy is difficult where shame is present.[2]

All lack of intimacy is not a result of personal shame. Yet it often is the undoing of relationships within families. It affects not only the relationship of a man with his wife, but with other men who are friends, and most of all with a man's own children.

Donald is 30 years old, and like most men has vivid memories of his father. He shared his memories with me. He was four or five years old, when one night his mother said, "Donny, it is time to go to bed." He said he ran to his father for a good-night kiss. When he got there his dad put his hand on his chest to hold him back, and said, "We are too old for that."

When he was eleven years old his family went to see his father's mother and father. Donald said he was the first out of the car, and up the steps to the front door where he was met by his grandmother. They threw their arms around each other and she gave him a big hug. He then looked up and there was his grandfather, whom he had not seen in over six years. He ran to him and his grandfather put his hand to his chest, held him back and said, "We are too old to do that." He said, "I then remembered my father's same gesture several years before."

This is a serious problem. Fathers do not know how to be intimate with their own children. The same pattern of aloneness or aloofness is passed on—particularly to sons.

Why Are Men That Way?

Fathers often will not or cannot bless their children because of their lack of intimacy with them.

Men today have forgotten that God has called them to *restore the power of* His kingdom. They have become less than strong, vibrant role models for their sons. There are two models that many men emulate today. One is the TV macho Rambo man, taking the world by violence. The other is the effeminate man, emasculated by the feminists. Many of these were wounded by abusive fathers or uncles and are striking back at all men with their inordinate behavior.

There is certainly nothing wrong with a man who can cry, hold a baby, do household chores, and be sensitive to his wife and children. Such a man is more genuine a man than the "super-macho" who beats his wife and/or abuses his children.

What happens so frequently is that men mistake *sensitivity for passiveness.* So to be politically correct, these men abdicate their place of leadership not only in the marketplace but in their own homes.[3]

There are also those who have spent their young lives challenging all authority and power. They have now grown up not only suspicious of authority in others, but afraid to exercise it themselves. When men abdicate the biblical role of priest in their homes, a vacuum is created. Wherever a vacuum exists, demons can rush in to fill it.

Many men act the way they do because they feel *dispensable or outmoded*. Feeling unneeded or inadequate can be resolved when men understand their position in God's plan for the family.

Lack of understanding of their godly role in the family results in *low self-esteem and fear*. These feelings have led many men to crawl into a shell, becoming oblivious to their responsibilities. They often shut up their hearts and close their mouths. This not only affects them profoundly, but the next generation is severely wounded.

When Men Don't Talk

One of the weaknesses of our culture is the inability of men to converse with one another. That is, conversation about life, other not just jock talk, cars, sports, and the latest joke. Even important subjects like marriage, sex, and relationships are often spoken of on the lighter side rather than the serious. For years men have been encouraged to talk to their wives, to spend quality time in intimate communication. This is essential to a healthy marriage.

But there is something that men need from other men that they cannot find from their wives. They need friendship with other men—someone they can bear their heart to. Someone who will hold them accountable. If temptation comes, they can share their heart for understanding and prayer.

Mentors are wonderful. So are spiritual leaders. But a relationship with another man who is a trusted friend can help an individual immeasurably. I recently met two men who told me they had been friends for twenty-five years. Finally, they broke down the barriers of pride, fear, and mistrust, and for the first time in their lives they are finding answers together for their marriages, their grandchildren, and for the declining years of their lives. They were overjoyed when I verified that what they were doing is possibly the best thing that could be happening in their lives.

One trait that has a singular impact upon succeeding generations is a man's hesitation to share his soul. Men have a very difficult time talking about their hurts, their desires, and their dreams. If they could just learn to tell their life stories, these thoughts and feelings would surface. Wives and children can't hear what men do not say.

George Steel was 40 years old. He was considered withdrawn and a bit indifferent by his family. His three sons were the joy of his life. His face brightened as he shared with me about Scott, the oldest. How responsible he was—he even had a job in a grocery store when he was in the seventh grade. Scott was like a second father to Jason and Michael, his younger brothers.

George then started telling me about Jason, the basketball player. He was captain of his junior high team, star of the team in high school, and now on an athletic scholarship to the state university. When he started telling me about broken records and statistics, I realized this could go on for a long time, so I asked him about Michael.

He hesitated for a moment, and then said, "Well, Michael is different." I waited for him to tell me why he was different, but nothing came. He just took a step backward and said nothing.

I said, "George, you know brothers can be as different as night and day." He still did not say anything, but I noticed a look of sadness pass over his face. I probed a little by saying, "He has two pretty tough acts to follow."

Then George said, "That is not really it. I never expected the boys to all act alike. I just do not know how to handle Michael."

I said, "What do you mean? Does he get in a lot of trouble?"

"Oh no," replied George, "he is a good boy, maybe too good."

Then he completely changed the subject. "My dad was a coal miner back in Pennsylvania. He worked hard, and would come home tired and dirty. We always had to be quiet so he could rest. I remember one holiday he dug out his old flat baseball glove and played catch with my sister and me." Then he said, "Michael is always hanging on me and hugging me. Frankly, I'm worried that he will not grow up to be a real man."

I decided to hit it head on. "George, are you worried that Michael could be too effeminate or maybe even homosexual?"

The pained look came across his face again and he said, "His mother does a lot better with him than I do."

"George," I asked, "Tell me about your dad. What was he like?"

"He was tall, which is probably where Jason gets his good height for basketball. His hands were rough from working in the mines, and he limped from an accident that had happened down in a mine a long time ago. I hated the mines. My dad was always tired and didn't have time for the family. That is why my wife and I moved to the West as soon as we could."

"Tell me, George, what was the best moment with your dad that you can remember."

"Oh, I suppose that day he played catch with my sister and me."

"What was the most painful memory you have of your dad?"

He replied without hesitation, "That same day, I got so excited about playing catch with dad, that for the first time I ran to hug him, and he turned his back. We were both embarrassed."

Then I said, "George, it sounds to me like the men in your family do not know how to say what they feel very well. Michael really wants you to hug him and tell him you love him. In fact, the very concern you have for him will only get worse if you do not begin to show your love and acceptance of him. You might try this with those other boys of yours too. Even though Scott is married, he needs to be shown that fathers and sons can have intimate feelings. You cannot really *bless* your boys until this happens."

When George finally saw the complete picture he did a marvelous turnaround with his sons.

All three of them always loved their father tremendously and wanted to please him. Now it was as if they were released from jail, and finally could be what they were created to be. It wasn't until George overcame some of the family culture and tradition that he was able to get close to each boy in an intimate way.

Now the blessing for each began to pour out. Scott and Jasonare well on their way to fine careers and wonderful families. Michael will always be the sensitive, caring person that God made him to be. He and his wife recently became youth pastors at a thriving church. George and his wife Sue, are basking inthe closeness of their family, with much to teach the new generation that is arriving.

I have found that fathers and sons often do not talk to one another about what is closest to their hearts. Yet when they do, a bond grows between them. There is a question that I have asked dozens of men: "What one response would you like to have received from your dad?" The overwhelming reply was, "That he would have spent more time talking to me."

Sons should be encouraged to ask their fathers questions. Fathers and grandfathers want to be approached even if they don't seem to want this. When they are, and when they start sharing their stories a bond begins to develop. Something else begins to happen in both hearts. A considerable forgiveness takes place when a father is asked about himself, about his life. He accepts himself then and is free to share his life experiences.

In the book *Iron John* by Robert Bly, Michael Mead interviewed men who served in the Gulf War and found that many had not heard their own grandfather's stories about World War II. The same phenomenon was revealed earlier when men who came back from the Vietnam War were interviewed.

The WW II veterans had returned from a savage, hideous, and horrifying war and felt they were not supposed to talk about it. Many had never even told their wives what happened to them and their buddies. It is a serious problem if they don't tell their sons (and daughters) before they are asked to go to war themselves. What accounts for this silence? Are American men afraid to share their deepest hurts and experiences?[4]

Robert Bly says that in Russia the older men take aside their young people from time to time strictly for "soul-talk." This is a time for sharing stories, the past, and inner thoughts. He says we do not even have a word in our vocabulary for "soul-talk." In fact, the opposite seems to be true in our society. A young man named Frank said, "There was always a stiffness in the air when my father and I were in the same room. It was like two people at a party, but no one had introduced us to each other."

There is something about the birth of the firstborn child into a family that remains a mystery. It is so wonderful, so mysterious, so miraculous, and yet so frightening. For a young father this experience is comparable to standing on a 200-foot tower, with the bungee cord around his body. You want to jump, but because you have never jumped it before you are not sure that it won't kill you. Or at least scare the living daylights out of you! And just before you jump, everyone leaves you alone. You wonder. *Who is going to say it is all right? Who is going to tell me when to jump? Or not to jump!* How many young men are abandoned at the moment of their own becoming a father, by their own father? Very few fathers give the emotional and physical support to their sons that is needed at this crucial time. In possibly the most emotional moment of the father-son relationship, when the son becomes a father, most American men are abandoned.

I hear someone saying, "Wait a minute, what about his wife, isn't she is the one having the baby?" Yes, I will grant you that. But that is primarily the problem. Men are taught to believe that the woman is the childbearer, the life-giver, the sole link between the past and the future. Physiologically this is true, but the young father is also responsible for this life. Genetically, spiritually, and morally he must take on the awesome responsibility of high priest in the family. The power of God's kingdom will be given or denied according to his faith and actions What tremendous strength and direction he would feel if his own father would just be there to guide him through the process.

I began asking men if their fathers were with them at the birth of their firstborn children. I found that in most cases, their fathers were not present. My conclusion is that most men never learn how to help their sons become men, because their own fathers did not help them.

Most of this deficit in training originates because of inadequate communication between parent and child, specifically between fathers and sons.

Here are some conclusive effects of fathers talking regularly with their children.

- *Identity*—Children gain a significant understanding

of who they are—their origin, their history, their ancestry, and their peculiarities.

- *Bonding*—Genetic similarities are insignificant compared to the spiritual and soul-bonding that transpires through hours of sharing in meaningful conversation.

- *Forgiveness*—It does not matter what discipline has been endured, what disappointment has been suffered, what has been missed or undone—communication through words, touching, and physical presence, create the most potent forgiving climate in all of life. Parents who discipline their children either physically or emotionally, do an enormous disservice to their children if they subsequently desert them verbally.

- *Blessing*—A blessing is not complete until it is spoken. And it is easier for a son or a daughter to receive a blessing from their parents if they are familiar with the voice, that is, they have experienced identity, bonding, and forgiveness through that parent.

The Bonding Process

In my experience of counseling hundreds of men over the years, I am convinced that by-and-large men are what they are because of their father's influence, good or bad.

The father figure is every man's masculine "root" in this world. Men who have been alienated from their father, bear a burden almost too heavy to carry. The result of father-son alienation is the breeding-ground for the destruction of an individual, a family, and even the society.

Tim was forty-seven when he told me his story of growing up in a dysfunctional home with a father who was always angry. He shared how his father directed that anger at his family until every relationship was in peril. His father was often verbally abusive to his mother, and sometimes physically violent. Tim said that more often than not he became the target of his father's anger. He never knew why, but in those early years he often wondered what it was that made his dad so upset.

One day they were up on the roof. It had been leaking and Tim and his dad were putting tar under the shingles and nailing them down. He watched his dad take a big swing at a nail and come down directly on his thumb. Tim said his dad jumped up and started dancing around until he thought he would fall off the roof. The air became heavy as he began to swear, using every word in his vocabulary, of foul language.

To a twelve-year old boy it was funny, and Tim said that he just snickered a little and probably smiled. His father looked up just in time to see that smile and he became even more angry. He still had the hammer in his hand, and as hard as he could throw it, he hurled it at Tim's head. Tim was fortunate that his dad's anger ruined his aim and he missed, but the memory has stayed with Tim for thirty years.

His dad is dead now, but Tim recalls the night he discovered the source of his father's anger. Tim was a fine basketball player. The night that he was to be awarded honors for being the best free-throw shooter on the team, everything came to a head. It was Tim's chance to have his parents see him receive the awards he'd worked for. But just before they were to leave for the award presentation, his parents got into a terrible argument. Tim remembers them shouting at each other and carrying on for some time. Then, suddenly his dad was gone, and his mother said out of the blue, "I suppose he went back to his first wife." Tim was shocked. He had never known that his dad had been married before. So here he was, sixteen years old, going off alone to be honored for the one thing he was good at.

Tim said that several years later he found out the whole

story. His dad was about eighteen years old when a teenage girl came to his home and accused him, in front of his mother, of being the father of her unborn baby. His mother demanded to know the truth. When Frank admitted that he had an intimate relationship with the girl, his mother said, "You are going to marry her!"

Tim said that the marriage did not last very long, but his parents kept the truth from their children all those years. He said, he knew that his dad's whole life was affected by this sin and the manner in which it was dealt with, and that he had never been able to resolve all the anger in his life.

It is evident that nearly every incident in a person's life, whether it is negative or positive, has potential to affect the next generation. There is only one way to change history, and that is to have past sins forgiven through the blood of Christ. Each sin can be removed as we find forgiveness and as we forgive those who have sinned against us. *"For if you live according to the sinful nature, you will die; but if by the Spirit you put to death the misdeeds of the body, you will live, ... For you did not receive a spirit that makes you a slave again to fear, but you received the Spirit of sonship. And by him we cry, 'Abba, Father'." Romans 8:13-15.*

I have found that inside every five-hundred-dollar business suit, and every twenty-dollar pair of faded coveralls, can be found the wounded heart of a son longing for the acceptance of love from his daddy! Of course there are exceptions, but where there has been neglect and rejection, the anger, pain, and frustration seldom completely disappear. The only answer is the bonding process from father to son through God the Father and His son Jesus Christ.

"But when the time had fully come, God sent his Son, born of a woman, born under law, to redeem those under law, that we might receive the full rights of sons. Because you are sons, God sent the Spirit of his Son into our hearts, the Spirit who calls

out, *"Abba, Father." So you are no longer a slave, but a son; and since you are a son, God has made you also an heir"* Galatians 4:4-7.

Men without role-model fathers, or fathers who have not shown them how to move from adolescence to manhood, eventually bond with another image. Some will bond with feminists, who were also hurt by parents or others who were abusive, absent, or otherwise unconcerned with their lives.

Richard Dalby, in his book *Fathers and Sons*, notes that many of the young men who join gangs do so because they do not have a father. Here they receive acceptance, affirmation, and male instruction. Here they also learn how to substitute violence for power. Fathers must understand this truth: You empower your son to "be." You give him credence to be a man, a husband, a father, a responsible person, a caring person, and other qualities that make up a God-fearing law-abiding citizen.

Dalby records how a sister who was doing prison work was asked by a young prisoner to get him a card to send his mom for Mother's Day. When the other men found out about this, they started asking her to get them cards. She went to a greeting card company and was able to obtain several crates of them. Knowing that Father's Day was not far away she asked the card company for a crate of Father's Day cards. Then she learned a very frightening and revealing fact: Not one of the men asked her for a card to send to his father. She was forced to assume that most of these men did not have a role-model or any meaningful relationship with their father.

Fathers are responsible not only for bringing babies into this world, but also for helping to take them from childhood to manhood. This has been left to mothers far too many times. Men who have abandoned their wives and families, leave that son in a position of vulnerability, either to be initiated into manhood by a gang, or non-caring adults, or not at all. There are 40 and 50-year-olds all around us who have never been initiated into manhood. The immaturity and childishness is evident in these woeful individuals.

The sad burden and concern for most boys who have been abandoned by their fathers, is that their mother has also been abandoned by their father. Dalby says, "The finest woman's best is not good enough to usher a boy into manhood." The wisdom of the ages, and modern family experts say that at some point the umbilical cord between mother and son must be severed. This is why primitive cultures separate the boys from their mothers for six months to a year in an initiation process.

Sometimes the mother and son do not know if they will ever see each other again. It has nothing to do with the boy's love for his mother, or with her love for him. Usually their relationship following the initiation is different, but healthier. This experience can only be empowered by men in society.

Several years ago we had the honor of being invited to a young Jewish boy's Bar-Mitzvah. The whole ceremony was very meaningful and impressive. I will always remember the moment after the young man had quoted several passages of Scripture in the Hebrew language. His grandfather handed the Torah to the young man's father. He in turn handed it to the young initiate who quoted the Shema from *Deuteronomy 6:4: "Hear, O Israel: The Lord our God, the Lord is one."* He then said these words, *"I am proud to be a Jew."*

This was a significant and life-changing moment in that young man's life. The identification process was never more clear. His heritage, starting with Abraham and Moses, moving through his grandfather, then his father, was now resident in his own life.

Is it possible that we have wanted to get so far away from the rituals of the High Church that we have missed some very powerful acts and expressions of bonding and blessing?

One of the glaring defects of our culture and our church is that we have lost the importance of a significant initiation of young boys into manhood. Perhaps it can be inaugurated and developed as families catch the value of it for their sons. It is as one man in his forties said to me, "There was never a time in my life that I knew when I became a man. I wish my dad or someone would have anointed me in some way and said, "Jerry, you are now a man."

Here is a suggested initiation process that churches or men's groups could develop. (This can be done by a father for his son or daughter or for the child without a father.)

The Initiation Process

(A sample)

The write Preparation

1. Spend as many months (years) as possible telling the stories of the family.

2. Make plans for the special day and ceremony of initiation.

3. Write out your plans and agenda for making this happen.

The right Process

1. Use the Scripture. Have the initiate memorize appropriate passages.

2. Involve the whole family. Affirm the initiate in positive ways.

3. The umbilical cord needs to be cut by the mother, symbolically in some way.

4. Pass on a special symbol of the family—possi-

bly a family heirloom (a ring, a Bible, or other book or momento).

5. Be sure a verbal blessing is given by the parents.

The rite of Passage

1. Do not put too much pressure on him/her to change in any way.

2. Continue to validate his manhood—her womanhood.

3. He/she will need help through many difficult times—this is an ongoing process.

The Power Of Fatherhood

Men must learn how to be priests in their homes, the representatives of God himself to their children. Norma Radin, in *The Role of the Father in Child Development*, says, "One is left with the overall conclusion that in spite of the limitations in the state of our knowledge, a father influences his children's mental development through many and diverse channels: through his genetic background, through his manifest behavior with his offspring, through the attitudes he holds about himself and his children, through the behavior he models, through his position in the family system, through the material resources he is able to supply for his children, through the influence he exerts on his wife's behavior, through his ethnic heritage, and through the vision he holds for his children. Finally, when he dies or separates from the family, the memories he leaves with his wife and children continue to exert an influence, perhaps equal to the impressions he made on the youngsters when he was physically present[6]."

How To Talk To Your Children

There are two concerns of parents, beyond teaching the

fundamentals of life to their children. Fathers must help them pass from adolescence to adulthood through constant guidance and affirmation. Secondly, both parents must pass on a blessing to each child, verbally as well as in action. This will allow the child to become an adult without the fear of never being accepted into the adult world. Confidence must be developed in them through the loving, encouraging parent. It will also release the child to be all that God wants him to be.

Both the "passage" and the blessing are unique. They may be separate or they may hinge upon each other. They will come about as parents are confident in themselves and know who they are, and that God has a plan for their children's lives.

Learn to talk to each child at an early age. Keep talking to them as they grow older. Tell them stories of the family, parents, and grandparents. Make your conversation include interesting gems from the past. Talk about little details to the little children because they identify with small things. Tell them about your feelings as a child, your fears, excitements, hobbies, interests, and sports. Share with them about your romance with their mother or father, as the case may be. Do not overdo it. Be brief and sensitive, but talk to them. And tell them that you love them. Never assume they know it without verbal confirmation.

How To Talk To Your Father

Fathers and sons must learn how to communicate with each other. Older men do not normally talk frankly about their marriage, or any other deep subject, with anyone, let alone their sons. If the son says, "Dad, let's spend a week together up in the mountains or at the shore," the father will likely say, "I don't have the time."

You may have to physically place your father in the car

and drive away. He may not speak for two days! You will need to ask the questions. When he does open up, you will find a bond and a healing take place in your lives unlike anything you have ever experienced.

Many sons have rare memories of fathers who spent a great amount of time with them just having fun. But most of the men in that category reveal that they had difficulty communicating with their fathers on a deep lever.

A man probably cannot have stronger feelings than those he has for his father. Yet those feelings are seldom expressed openly. I can count on one hand the number of times I have seen an athlete on TV say, "Hi, Dad," to the camera. Few men confess they have ever said, "I love you, Dad," no matter how much they would like to.

Keep in mind that your father may have never done this before. Remember your father is a son too. You are in a better position to take the initiative than he is. If sons and daughters do not start talking to their dads, that coveted conversation may never take place.

Never begin the conversation with grievances, even if they are justified. Start by asking about his childhood and the good times your own childhood has been with him. Do not interrupt or argue. Listen for dimensions of your dad that you did not know existed.

Search for common ground. Do not be afraid to tell him of your fond memories of times spent together. Tell him how much you need him and love him. It is so very important for your father to hear that *you love him.*

Some men put off telling their fathers they care about them until it is too late. "My only regret," Dwight Eisenhouer wrote shortly after his father died, "is that it was always so difficult to let him know the great depth of my affection for him."[7]

Randy was 42 years old when he waited at his dying father's bedside. He was hoping he would hear, "I love you, Randy," before his father died. He never heard the words. He told me with tears in his eyes, "I dream of hearing those words from my fahter. Oh how I wish he had said them."

Questions For Sons To Consider

1. Using one to ten words, describe your relationship with your father.

2. What was one response you wanted from your dad that you never received?

3. How are you like your dad?

4. In one word, how would your children describe you?

I never met a man who at the end of his life said, "God, I wish I had spent more time at the office." Tim Hansel[8]

"See, I will send you the prophet Elijah before that great and dreadful day of the Lord comes. He will turn the hearts of the fathers to their children, and the hearts of the children to their fathers; or else I will come and strike the land with a curse" (Malachi 4:5-6).

Chapter Twelve

Moving Ahead To Victory
It Is Time to Begin

God has never required perfection in His children. Perfection may be the target we shoot for, but it is not a prerequisite to Christian success. It is the eternal goal of mankind, but no one except Jesus has ever reached it in this life.

The eminent message of Christianity is not perfection, or holiness, or even righteousness. The principle theme of Christ's redeeming work for mankind is *Grace*. *"for it is by grace you have been saved, through faith—and this not from yourselves, it is the gift of God"* (Ephesians 2:8).

I have sinned. Even after I accepted Christ I sinned. The majestic hope of my soul is not that I must be perfect, but God in His infinite mercy and love provides compassionate grace, and unfathomable forgiveness.

My family is not perfect. In spite of imperfections we have been blessed, and nearly all of my father's descendants are following Christ. We thank God daily for His mercy and pray that His covenant blessing of grace and protection will cover each member of our family.

One significant truth I know: When I fail as a man, father, husband, grandfather, pastor, and Christian, through Christ I can find forgiveness and strength and direction.

Do not be discouraged if you have fallen short of your goals. Do not give up on your family if you have failed them. Do not think that it will never work. Do not think that you will never be able to bless your children and see them consistently following God's path.

God is faithful. He never goes back on His covenant. He will forgive you and give you strength to carry on.

Start a *generational blessing*. The time to start is today.

Fathers help *initiate your sons into manhood*. Remember, this is as much a spiritual issue as a physical one.

Jellybean Revisited

My grandson Jordan and I drove down the street where the infamous Jellybean had met his demise. I asked Jordan if he could see the spot where Jellybean had laid so long. We looked as closely as we could. There, after two years, we could see just a faint lightness in the coat of paint in the shape of the dead, flattened, forgotten, painted-over possum. I reminded Jordan how neglected sin makes such a mark so deep that even when it is gone we sometimes see the scars.

In all of his nine-year-old wisdom, he replied, "But

Papa, he is gone, and we will never have to look at him again."

Postscript

Satan has a way of attacking Christians at their most vulnerable position. He has done this repeatedly throughout our ministry. If Mardell and I were going to speak at a couple's retreat, or a Valentine banquet, invariably our differences in opinion would be magnified just before the occasion.

Several times as I prepared to preach on healing, or before I was to pray for an ill person, I would find myself battling symptoms that would not only test my physical endurance but my faith.

Shortly after I began the writing of this book, Satan once again came with his big guns blazing and his panzer division roaring. Just before Thanksgiving of 1992, our oldest daughter, Danell, learned that she had a malignant lump in one of her breasts.

Knowing that it was going to be a troubled Christmas time for those of us in Oregon, our youngest daughter, Lynne, her husband, Jonathan, and their three sons came out from Iowa to celebrate the holidays with us. To say the least, these were difficult times as Danell faced surgery, chemotherapy, and radiation.

We are not superstitious people, but one day as Mardell and I were in pain for Danell, I said, "Isn't it what Satan always does to us? He attacks us where he can hurt us the most. Maybe I should quit talking about this generational blessing and not finish the book."

Mardell replied, "Don't you think that is exactly what Satan wants you to do?"

One day Danell was going through the agony of all the poison that they were putting into her body. I put my arms around her and said, "Danell, I'm so sorry, I wish I could do this for you." She turned to me and said, "It's okay, Dad, all Satan can do is destroy my body, he can't touch my soul." I wept as I realized that is really what it is all about. He can attack our earthly home, but with Christ living there, he cannot destroy the person within.

We are praising God! Danell came through the surgery, chemotherapy, and radiation. It was not always easy, but with the struggle comes growth. Praise God, He gives us the victory!

Endnotes

Chapter 1
1. Pierson Parker, *Inherit the Promise* (Greenwich, Conn.: The Seabury Press, 1957)

Chapter 2
1. Leonard Ravenhill, *America Is Too Young to Die* (Minneapolis: Bethany House Publishers,1979).
2. John DeVries, School on New Age Movement
3. Timothy Leary, *Flashbacks* (Los Angeles J. B. Tarcher, Inc. 1983) p.260

Chapter 3
1. Thomas B. White, *The Believers Guide To Spiritual Warfare* (Ann Arbor, Mich.: Servant Publications, 1990)
2. Fred Dickason, *Demon Possession and the Christian*, (Chicago: Moody Press, 1987)
   Notes: Elwell, *Evangelical Dictionary of Theology* (Grand Rapids, Mich.· Baker Book House).

Demonize—A distinction is made between demon possession and demonic influence, with the one being possessed called an "energumen". Some understood the demonic influence to include the inducement of evil thoughts directly into the minds of men, (Augustine, Athanasius, Origen, Peter Lonbard, Bede, Thomas Aquinas). This form of temptation was considered to be the demon's normal mode of operation, while possession was recognized as only an extraordinarily strong extension of a demon's control over man. Unger, Dr. Merrial, *Demons in the World Today* (Wheaton, Ill.: Tyndale House, 1971). He states that a non-Christian can be totally controlled and manipulated by demonic power. A Christian rarely has the same degree of complete subjugation. (I take this position, although I have known of those who were Christians who exposed themselves to Satan so overtly that they became possessed.) To be demonized, in my understanding, is to be so beat upon by Satan's demons that even a Christian loses the "Joy of His Salvation." One is still a Christian, but the attack has immobilized that person to near ineffectiveness.

3. Dr. Merrial Unger, *What Demons Can Do to Saints* (Chicago: Moody Press, 1977)
4. *60 Minutes*, T V Program, August 31, l992

Chapter 4
1. Thomas B. White, *The Believers Guide to Spiritual Warfare*, Ann Arbor, Mich.: Servant Publications, 1990).

Chapter 5
1. Leonard Ravenhill, *America Is Too Young to Die*, (Minneapolis: Bethany House Publishers, 1979), p. 112
2. Scott Walker, *The Freedom Factor: Overcoming the Barriers to Being Yourself*, (San Francisco: Harper and Row, l989).
3. Ibid.

Chapter 6
1. *The Encyclopedia of Religion*, Vol. 2, (New York: MacMillan and Free Press, 1987).
2. C. C. Brown, "The Many Facets of Touch" Johnson and Johnson Baby Products Co., 1984 ed.
3. Jillyn Smith, *Senses and Sensibilities*, (New York: John Wiley & Sons, Inc. 1989).
4. Ibid.
5. N. Stein, and M. Sanfililipo. "Depression and the wish to Be Held" - J Clin. Psychol. 41: 3-9, 1985
6. A. Finlayson, "The Healing Touch", Maclean's 98:68, Dec 9, 1985.
7. A. L. Steward, and M. Lupfer, "Touching as Teaching" - J. Appl. Soc. Psychol. 17: 800-809, 1987.

8. C. H. Anderson, and R. V. Heckel, "Perceptual and Motor Skills" 1985 60: 289-290

Chapter 7
1. Smally & Trent, *The Blessing*, (Nashville: Thomas Nelson Pub, 1986).
2. Kathleen McGuire, Workshops On Positive Discipline for Birth to Three.
3. The Encyclopedia of Religion, Vol. 2, New York: MacMillan & Free Press, 1987).
4. Ibid.

Chapter 8
1. Marilee Pierce Dunker, *Man of Vision, Woman of Prayer,* (Nashville: Thomas Nelson, 1980).
2. John and Paula Sanford, *Healing the Wounded Spirit,* (South Plainfield, N. J.: Bridge Publishing, Inc., 1985).

Chapter 9
1. USA Today, Newspaper, August 2, 1993.

2.Les Breitman, M. D. is a full-blooded Jew, raised traditionally in a reformed Jewish family—a very poor immigrant family from Russia. A medical doctor with extensive legal training, he became wealthy according to the basic convictions under which he was raised. After retiring at an early age, Les then came to find himself watching the movie, *The Late Great Planet Earth.*

He emerged in a state of shock. What if Hal Lindsey and his interpretation of biblical prophecy was correct? Then Les, in spite of all his wealth, was actually wasting his life and would pay the price throughout eternity! What a frightful thought!

Les then began a study of Bible prophecy. Ultimately, he decided to read the Bible. But to him, a Jew, there was only one book—the Old Testament. The New Testament was for the "goyim"—the gentiles. He began to read. But unbeknownst to him, the Holy Spirit was leading Les into an abounding understanding of all the Old Testament Scripture that foretold of the coming of Jesus, the Messiah. Les simply could not understand, at that time, why he was comprehending the 317 prophecies concerning Jesus, whereas his forefathers and his contemporary Jewish brethren failed to see the relevance.

After Les finished the Old Testament, he felt as though he had read a wonderfully revealing instuctrional book, but somehow he had left out the last chapter. So he turned that fateful page and began to read the Gospel of Matthew. He just couldn't stop; he continued to read those wonderful, perfect, logical, and flawless words written in red letters! He finished the New Testament in just a few days, and demonstrating that there is surely power in the Gospels, he believed, and he tearfully, joyously fell to his knees and accepted Jesus as his Lord and Savior.

Dr. Breitman and his wife Linda live in Denver. God is using Les to lecture about Jewish customs and how they relate to the imminent return of Jesus; i.e., the Jewish betrothal and wedding, and the seven Israelite festivals of Leviticus 23, and how they are fulfilled to the letter by Jesus.

3.*Homosexuality* by Dr. Les Breitman—A 1987 study revealed that 23% of the sexual partners of HIV-infected men became infected after one year of sexual activity, despite having used condoms every time. Why? Because latex condoms contain microscopic holes called "intrinsic voids," measuring 4 microns in size. But the HIV virus is only .1 to .3 microns in diameter. That means that the microscopic hole is from 17 to 50 times larger than the HIV virus itself, permitting free passage of the virus anywhere that it finds one of these holes. Conclusion: Condoms do not prevent transmission of the HIV virus. They only forestall infection for a matter of months. This is like playing Russian roulette with three bullets in the revolver instead of one. It is also like trying to stop a .22 bullet with a chain-link fence!

Amebiasis is one of the several diseases spread via anal sex— a deviant activity practiced by homosexual men. It is a severe intestinal ailment with dire complications that can also be spread by food handlers infected with this protozoan microorganism. During the 1967-69 period of burgeoning sexual liberation, the incidence of amebiasis increased at 50 times the normal incidence in the San Francisco homosexual community. This is in addition to the increased incidence of hepatitis-B and HIV infections. By the end of the 1970's, during the era of the "gay bathhouses, homosexual men made 80% of the 70,000 annual visits to the city's STD clinics." (David Horowitz, *The Queer Fellows*, American Spectator, January 1993, p. 46)

Chapter 10
1. Marilyn Fergeson, *The Aquarian Conspiracy*, St. Martins Press, 1980.
2. John Dumphy, "The Humanist" Magazine, 1982.
3. Richard Beswick, "The New Age in Education & Education 2000: An Integrated Curriculum" - An Interim Report to the Education Project, 1990.
4. Ibid
5. Ibid
6. Phil Phillips, *Saturday Morning Mind Control*, (Nashville: Thomas Nelson Publishers, 1991).

7. Peter Leithart & George Grant, A Christian Response to Dungeons and Dragons, (Fort Worth, Tx.: Dominion Press).
8. John DeVries & Erwin Lutzer, *Satan's Evangelistic Strategy For The West*, (Wheaton, Il.: Victor Books, 1989).
9. John DeVries, School on the New Age.

Chapter 11

1. Mircea Eleade, *Rites and Symbols of Initiation*, (New York: Harper and Row, 1975).
2. Gordon Dalby, *Father and Son*, (Nashville: Thomas Nelson, Publishers, 1992).
3. Ibid
4. Robert Bly, *Iron John*, (New York: Vintage Books, Random House, Inc., 1990).
5. Warren Farrell, *The Myth of Male Powers*, (New York: Simon and Schuster, 1993).
6. Norma Radin, *The Role of Fathers in Child Development*, John Wiley and Sons Inc., 1981
7. Ralph Keyes, *Sons on Fathers: A Book of Men's Writing*, Harper and Collins, 1992
8. Tim Hansel, *What Kids Need Most in a Dad*, (Old Tappen, N. J.: Fleming H. Revell, Co., 1984 - 1989).

Dan LeLaCheur pastored churches for thirty years. He presently is vice-president of Development at Eugene Bible College in Eugene, Oregon. He and his wife Mardell conducted seminars on the family for several years. They had a call-in radio program in Des Moines, Iowa called Family survival, and a television interview program with the same name. Dan spends a great amount of time speaking at retreats, conferences, and churches, on the subject of Breaking Generational Curses, and Starting Generational Blessings.

Those wishing to contact Dan LeLaCheur for speaking engagements, or to order books may do so at the following address.

Dan LeLaCheur
Family Survival Ministries
P.O. Box 2114
Eugene, OR 97402

Book Price - $8.99

Postage and Handling - 1st. book / $1.50
Each additional book / $1.00

Leaders Guide - $4.95

With an order for four books a *Leaders Guide for Generational Legacy* may be requested and will be sent free of charges.

Notes

Notes

Notes